The Best Way to Learn Chinese Chess or XiangQi for Beginners

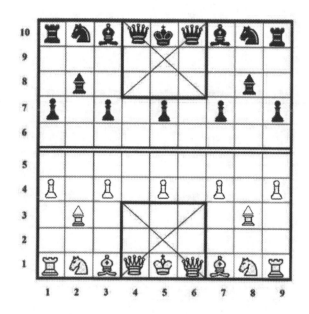

Norman Chan

authorHOUSE®

AuthorHouse™
1663 Liberty Drive
Bloomington, IN 47403
www.authorhouse.com
Phone: 1 (800) 839-8640

Published by AuthorHouse 12/04/2018

ISBN: 978-1-5462-6945-8 (sc)
ISBN: 978-1-5462-6944-1 (e)

Print information available on the last page.

This book is printed on acid-free paper.

PREFACE

In popular culture, the travels of Marco Polo brought together the civilizations of West and East. The cultural exchanges that followed continue to enrich the lives of people around the world.

Chinese Chess or "Xiangqi", a board game that is very popular in China and Asia, is a very fascinating and strategic cousin of "universal" Chess that we are playing around the world.

Using the innovative EZChess Board with ninety (90) squares ("universal" Chess is with sixty-four squares); and an invented "coordinates" move-recording system, I have introduced an enhanced version of this majestic ancient game. I hope my readers who, with some basic "universal" chess skills and coordinates knowledge, can learn the complex Chinese Chess easily.

In chapter 2, my illustrative games are based on two games played a few hundred years ago in China. In chapter 5, I used the opening names and systems translated from the Chinese openings. In chapter 6, the "Special Rules" are current international Chinese Chess (or Xiangqi) rules used outside of China (China has a more strict rules). In chapter 7, the strategies and tactics of the mid-games are from my own experiences. In chapter 8, the fourteen (14) Grand Masters I listed are the elite groups of players during the last 60 years in the Chinese Chess history.

ACKNOWLEDGEMENTS

To my Family

A special gratitude to James Chan, Alex Chan, Christopher Chan and
Kayleigh Risser (Co-Editor)

My appreciation to my fellow "masters" of the game: Colin Cheng,
Mark Ma, John Mou, Oscar Peng and Mark Sokoll, PengYuan Chen and MingJiang Zheng

CONTENTS

CHAPTER 1   INTRODUCTION

1   THE BOARD

D 1.1.1   "UNIVERSAL" CHESSBOARD

This is the "universal" Chessboard that all of us are familiar with.

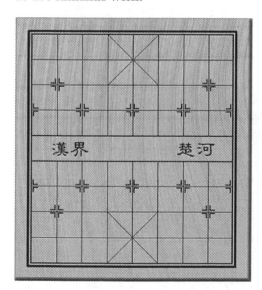

D 1.1.2   CHINESE CHESSBOARD

This is the "traditional" Chinese Chessboard or "Xiangqi" chessboard that is very popular and being played by millions of people in China, Vietnam, Asia nations and other countries.

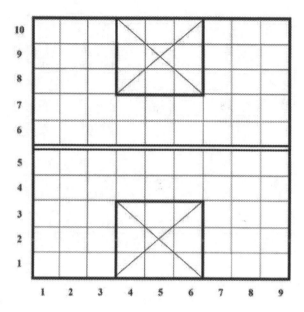

Patent Pending

D 1.1.3   NEW EZChess BOARD

This is the innovated 90-square chessboard or the new EZChess board that the author uses to teach the readers to learn Chinese Chess fast and easy.

1

2 THE OPENING POSITION

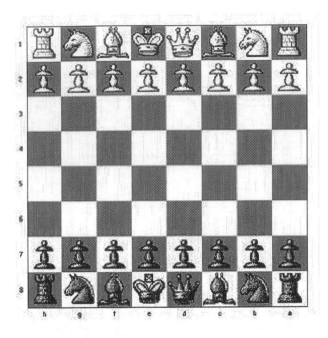

D 1.2.1 "UNIVERSAL" CHESS

This is a "universal" chessboard and 32 chessmen or pieces at their opening positions. This board is made up of 64 squares arrayed in an 8x8 grid of alternately colored squares.

There are 16 pieces on each side: 1 King, 1 Queen, 2 Rooks, 2 Knights, 2 Bishops and 8 Pawns. Pieces are in white and black colors.

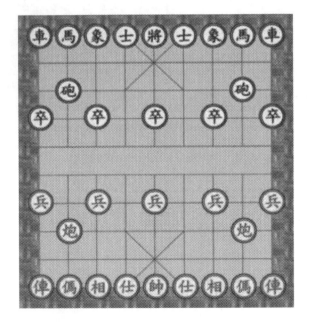

D 1.2.2 "TRADITIONAL" CHINESE CHESS OR XIANGQI

The diagram shows a traditional Chinese Chess or "Xiangqi" board with 32 chessmen or pieces at their opening positions. The board is made up of 9 vertical and 10 horizontal lines, create 90 intersection points. A river separates the two sides in the middle and one palace is on each side indicated with cross.

There are 16 pieces on each side, one side in red and other side in green or black. Each side has 1 General, 2 Chariots, 2 Horses, 5 Soldiers, 2 Ministers are named in red (and 2 Elephants in black), 2 Cannons and 2 Counselors (Advisors, Assistants or Guards). The pieces move from one intersection point to another intersection point.

D 1.2.3   NEW EZChess

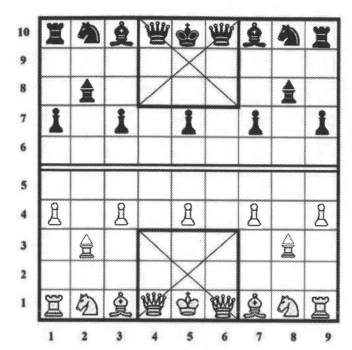

The diagram D1.2.3, created by the author, can help readers a fast and easy way to learn and appreciate the fantastic Chinese Chess game. The new innovative EZChess board is consisted of 90 squares in one color. Double border lines are in the middle and one palace is on each side.

There are 32 chessmen, or pieces, on the board at their opening positions, as shown in D1.2.3. The board has 9 columns, or files, and 10 rows, or ranks. The pieces move from one square to the others. There are 16 chessmen on each side: 1 King, 2 Rooks, 2 Knights, 5 Pawns, 2 Bishops, 2 Queens and 2 Cannons. The pieces are in red or white, and the other side is in black.

The arrangement of the opening position of the pieces is exactly the same as that of the traditional Chinese Chess. Instead of using the Chinese characters for the pieces, this author uses the "letters" to identify the pieces. All other pieces except the two Cannons and five Pawns are positioned in the back row or rank. The King is in the middle in 5th file, the two Rooks are on the outside corners, the Knights are next to the Rooks, the Queens are next to the King on both sides, and the Bishops are in-between the Queens and the Knights.

Please note that this author uses "Red" for all the "White" Pieces shown in the diagrams in this book.

3   THE NEW MOVE-RECORDING SYSTEM

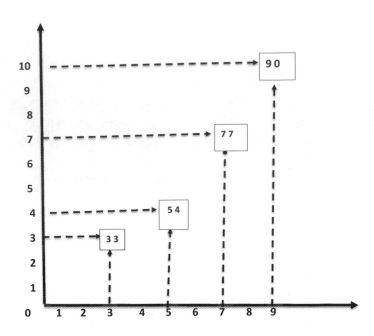

D 1.3.1

All ninety (90) squares on the EZChess Board are assigned a two-digit number.

Based on the system of coordinates commonly taught in school mathematics, the player picks the first digit number from the X-axis, or the horizontal numbers, and the second from the Y-axis, or the vertical numbers. For example: The number for Square 54 is made up with 5 from the 5th file, and 4 from the 4th rank; and square 90 is from the 9th file and the 10th rank. The "0" is used at "10th" Rank in order to make a single digit.

D 1.3.2

This diagram D1.3.2 shows all of the 90 two-digit numbers are printed on their designated squares.

The author's symmetrical system of movement-recording of the Chinese Chess pieces is an easier and more efficient mode of playing, since it is based on graph coordinates.

	1	2	3	4	5	6	7	8	9
10	10	20	30	40	50	60	70	80	90
9	19	29	39	49	59	69	79	89	99
8	18	28	38	48	58	68	78	88	98
7	17	27	37	47	57	67	77	87	97
6	16	26	36	46	56	66	76	86	96
5	15	25	35	45	55	65	75	85	95
4	14	24	34	44	54	64	74	84	94
3	13	23	33	43	53	63	73	83	93
2	12	22	32	42	52	62	72	82	92
1	11	21	31	41	51	61	71	81	91

4   THE PIECES

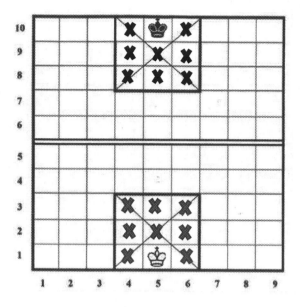

THE KING (K) ♔(Shuai) or (Jiang)

D 1.4.1

The King (The General in Chinese Chess), is the leader of his army or kingdom; his value is priceless. When the King is captured, the game is over! Whoever captures or stalemates the King first wins the game. The King can move only one square at a time, in any direction, and can only move inside his own Palace. He is prohibited to venture out of the Palace and he cannot move diagonally. The Diagram D1.4.1 indicates the nine squares in each Palace marked with crosses. The King can attack and capture a hostile piece in his movement range within the Palace.

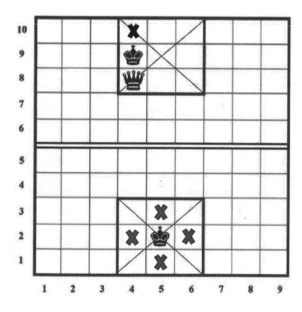

D1.4.2

This diagram shows a special rule or restriction for the two Kings in Chinese Chess; the Confrontation Rule. This rule states that the two Kings cannot confront each other and share the same file while there is/are no piece(s) between the Kings. The diagram D1.4.2 shows the White King is already in the King file, so the Black King cannot move into the King file, while the White King can move to the 4th file because there is a Queen in between them.

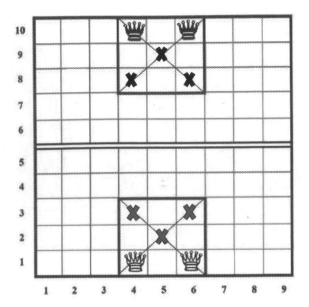

THE QUEEN (Q) ♛ (Shi)

D 1.4.3

There are two Queens (In Chinese Chess, they are Counselors, Assistants, Advisors or Guards) on each side. The Queen can only move diagonally in one direction and one square at a time and inside the Palace only. The King and the two Queens have to share the five squares indicated in the diagram in D1.4.3, marked with an "x". The Queen, like the King, can capture any enemy piece within its moving range in the Palace.

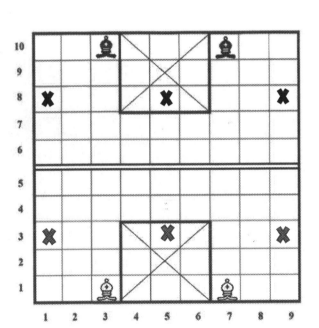

THE BISHOP (B) ♝ (Xiang)

D 1.4.4

There are two Bishops (In Chinese Chess, they are Ministers in white and Elephants in black) on each side. There is only one color on the Board, so there is no difference between the two Bishops. The Bishops can move in one direction, diagonally, two squares at a time. He cannot displace or leap over any other piece. There are seven squares (as marked with an "X" in the diagram D1.4.4) on each side. The Bishop is allowed to go in the Palace, but not to cross over the Border. The Bishop can capture enemy pieces only at the end-square of its move.

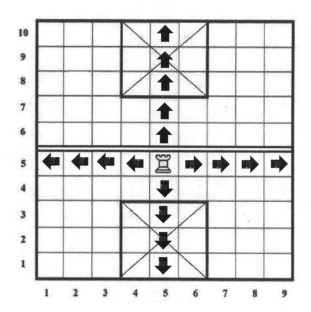

THE ROOK (R) ♖ (Ju)

D 1.4.5

The two Rooks (Chariots) on each side move and act like their counterparts in CHESS. The four Rooks are initially positioned at the four corner-squares of the board. A Rook can have a maximum 17 possible moves (squares). In the diagram D1.4.5, each arrow indicates a possible Rook's move. The Rook can capture enemy pieces that are within its moving range.

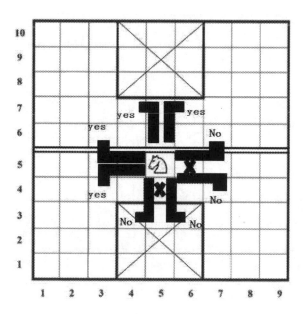

THE KNIGHT (N) ♘ (Ma)

D 1.4.6

There are two Knights (Horses) on each side. The Knight moves in the form of a capital "L" as exactly as his counterpart in CHESS. It can capture enemy pieces only at the end-square of its move. A Knight has a maximum of 8 possible squares to move into. The Knight is subject to an Obstruction Rule. On the diagram: when there is an "X" marked in a square next to a Knight (a piece @54 or @65 in the "long-leg" of the "L" path), then the Knight cannot move in that direction. The diagram D1.4.6 indicates only four squares (with "yes") in which the Knight @55 is free to move into.

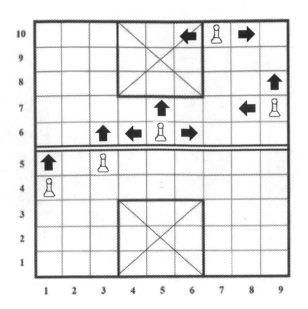

THE PAWN (P) (Bing) or (Zu)

D 1.4.7

There are five Pawns (Soldiers) on each side in Chinese Chess. The Pawn can only move forward one square at a time before and while crossing the Border (the River). After a Pawn crosses the Border, it attains better modes of attack and lateral movement except backward, (one square at a time always). Under no circumstance can the Pawn move diagonally, two squares jumping move, promotion to a Queen (or others), or capturing En Passant. A Pawn can attack any piece within his range.

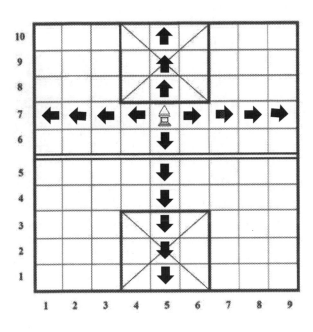

THE CANNON (C) (Pao)

D 1.4.8

There are two Cannons on each side in Chinese Chess. The Cannon moves in a similar fashion as the Rook, but in order to capture a hostile piece, he must leap over one piece (but no more than one), friendly or not. The piece attacked by a Cannon can be two squares or nine squares away.

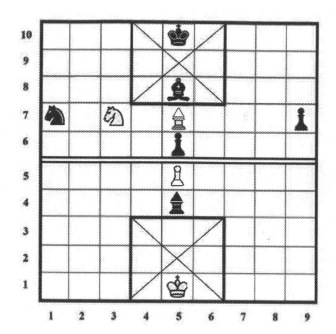

D 1.4.9 **CANNONS IN ATTACK**

The diagram D1.4.9 shows the white Cannon @57 is making a check on the Black King @50, and at the same time, he is attacking the Knight @17. The White Cannon @57 cannot attack the Black Cannon @54 because there are two pieces in between them, nor can he attack the edged Pawn @97 because there is no piece in between the two. Meanwhile, the Black Cannon @54 has nothing to do, and he cannot attack his own Pawn @56.

5   HOW MOVES ARE RECORDED

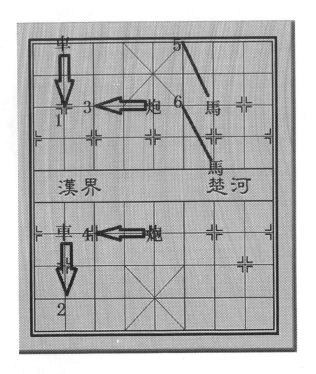

D 1.5.1 THE MOVE-RECORDING SYSTEMS USED IN "TRADITIONAL" CHINESE CHESS OR XIANGQI

In the Chinese Chessboard shown in D1.5.1, two Black Rooks are in the same file, one of them supposedly moves up two steps or intersections (R2+2), and both Rooks are qualified to do so. Which Rook? Is it the front Rook or the back Rook? The same confusion happens to the two Black Knights and two Black Cannons. Which Knight really moves back from the 7th file to 6th file (N7-6)? Which Cannon moves horizontally 2 steps or intersections from the 5th to 3rd file (C5=3)? They have to use "F" or "+" for the front, and "R", "B" or "—"for the back piece.

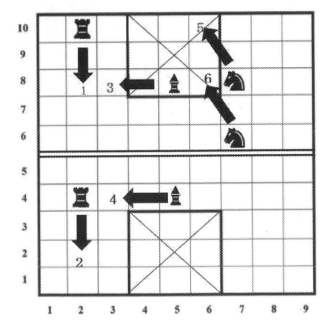

D 1.5.2

THE NEW MOVE-RECORDING SYSTEM USED IN THIS BOOK

The same positions are shown in the diagram D1.5.2. The innovative EZChess Board and the new move-recording system will clearly indicate the moves of all the Black pieces, shown in D1.5.1, without confusion or ambiguity.

In D1.5.2, The back Black Rook @20 moves up 2 squares to @28 (R2028), while the front Rook @24 moves up 2 squares to @22 (R2422). The back Black Cannon @58 moves 2 squares sideways to @38 (C5838), and the front Cannon @54 moves horizontally 2 squares to 34 (C5434). The back Black Knight @78 moves back to @60 (N7860), and the front Knight @76 moves back to @68 (N7668).

6 GENERAL RULES OF THE GAME

6.1 Object

The game is played by two persons. The player who checkmates the King or stalemates the opponent wins the game.

6.2 The Board and the Pieces

Each player should initially have sixteen pieces on the Board. Each side should have 1 King (General), 2 Queens (Counselors), 2 Bishops (Ministers in Red, Elephants in Black), 2 Rooks (Chariots), 2 Knights (Horses), 5 Pawns (Soldiers) and 2 Cannons (Cannons).

6.3 Movement of the Pieces

The White side should make the first move. The persons shall play alternately, one move at a time. A piece can only be moved legally into either an unoccupied square or a square occupied by an opposing piece. A legal move cannot be retracted.

6.4 Completion of Move

A move is completed when the player has quitted the last piece of the play. A captured piece has to be removed from the Board immediately in order to complete the play.

6.5 Adjustment of the Pieces

The player may adjust one or more of the pieces after giving notice of his intention to do so, by requesting "I adjust" (or "Bye-Qi" in Chinese) politely prior to the adjustment. A player shall not adjust the opponent's pieces.

6.6 Touching Pieces

If the player touches:

> A) One of his or her pieces, the piece has to be moved.
> B) One of the opponent's pieces, the piece must be taken.
> C) One of his or her own pieces, and one of the opponent's pieces, the latter must be taken with the former, if legal.

6.7 Illegal Moves

An illegal move must be stopped immediately and retracted back to the original position. Refusing to stop the illegal move will result in forfeiting the game. Unlike CHESS, some perpetual attacks are considered illegal in Chinese Chess. (See Chapter 6 in this book for "the Special Rules")

7   CHECK ON THE KING

The King is in check when he is being attacked.

The capture of the King or a stalemate means the game is over.

When a player places a King in check, the person should say the word "check!" or "Jiang" (It means "Check" in Chinese) to his or her adversary gently.

When under a check, the player has only three options:

1. The King moves out of check.
2. The hostile piece that places the King in check must be captured.
3. A piece is placed to block and protect the King from attack.

Please be reminded that, in Chinese Chess or Xiangqi:

1. 1. The King cannot move diagonally to other squares.
2. 2. The King is prohibited to move out of the Palace.
3. 3. The King is not permitted to move to an open file already occupied by the other King due to the Confrontation Rule.
4. 4. A Stalemate means a checkmate.
5. 5. The Palace can be entered from all three sides by any pieces, friendly or unfriendly.
6. 6. A King can attack or capture other hostile pieces inside the Palace walls.

8   CHECK AND CHECKMATE

D 1.8.1   **CHECKMATE**

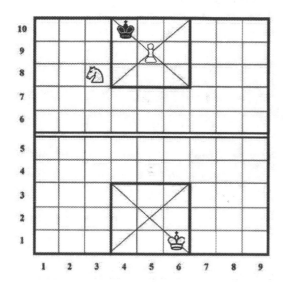

D 1.8.2   **THE CONFRONTATION RULE**

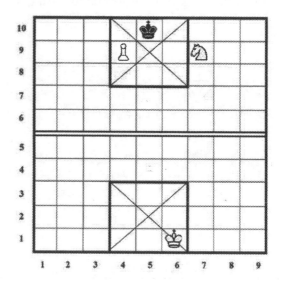

The Black King @40 is checkmated by the Knight @38. (The White Pawn @59 controls the @50 and @49 and the King has no place to hide inside the Palace).

The Black King @50 is checked by the Knight @79. The King could have moved to @60 but the "Confrontation Rule" prohibits him to go to @60 in the 6th File.

D 1.8.3   **STALEMATE**

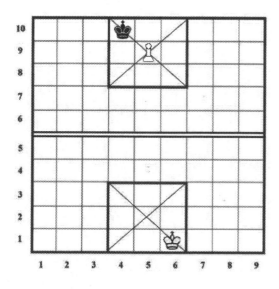

D 1.8.4   **PERPETUAL CHECK**

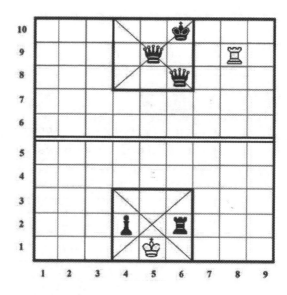

The Black King @40 has no place to escape. The helpless King has no men around to protect him. It is a stalemate! A stalemate in Chinese Chess means a checkmate.

1 R8980+ K6061, 2 R8089+ K6160, 3 R8980+ K6061
_ _ _ _ _

The White Rook @89 is making a perpetual check, which is an illegal move in Chinese Chess. White has to make the changes.

9 DRAWN GAMES

The game is drawn if one of the following requirements is met:

9.1 By Agreement

The players agree to a draw at any time during the game.

9.2 The 50-Move Rule (or an Agreed Number of Moves)

At any stage of the game, if fifty moves are played on each side without any captures occurring, then the game is a draw. The draw must be claimed as soon as the stipulated number of moves has been completed, and will not be allowed at any later period.

9.3 Insufficient Mating Material

When neither side is able to force a mate, the game is drawn.

9.4 Threefold Repetition

When the same position repeats three times consecutively, and the other side does the same, the game is drawn.

9.5 The Final Decision/Judgment from the Match Sponsor/Organization/Referee

When a dispute in the game happens, normally this is one of the last options.

NOTES:

1. **A Stalemate is not a draw, but a loss.**
2. **Perpetual Check is not allowed.**
3. **Some Perpetual Attacks are not permitted.**

> A Note to Our Readers: This author used RED for the WHITE PIECES for all diag. throughout this book

10 RELATIVE VALUES

NAME	SYMBOL		NO.	VALUE
Queen	♛	Q	2	1.0 points
Bishop	♝	B	2	1.0 points
Rook	♜	R	2	5.0 points
Knight	♞	N	2	2.5 points
Cannon	♟	C	2	2.5 points
Pawn	♟	P	5	1 to 2 points

The King is not assigned a value because he is priceless. His loss means the loss of the game. Many players consider the Knight and the Cannon are of the same value. Some may favor Cannons over Knights and vice versa. Many prefer Cannons over Knights in early games, and prefer Knights over Cannons in end games. A Rook's value is always higher than that of a Knight and a Cannon combined. The value of a Pawn keeps increasing as the game progresses.

There are different opinions on the comparative or relative values of Chinese Chess pieces. The author uses the most widely accepted one (not to get readers too confused on the values).

11   SELF-MADE NEW EZChess CHESS SET

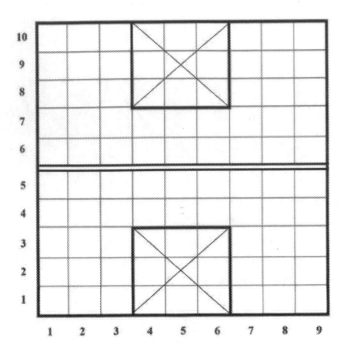

There is an easy and economical way for you to make the EZChess Board and Pieces for this game in minutes, by yourself. 1. Draw a 90-square board on a piece of white paper or on cardboard, using 10 vertical lines and 11 horizontal lines to make the 90 squares. 2. Take 2 sets of regular/universal chess sets. Borrow the Rooks and Queens from the 2nd set. 3. Turn the two Rooks upside down (in an inverted position) to be used as the Cannons. The new sets of this boards and pieces will soon be available for sales in stores.

12 CHESS NOTATION

A good move   !

A very good move   !!

A bad move   ?

A very bad move   ??

Check +

Checkmate   #

Stalemate   #

Loss due to time exhaustion   XX

Win by mutual agreement or abandonment of game *

Win by forfeiture resulted from violation of rules   **

A drawn game =

In a superior position   >

In a winning position   >>

And/or /

Play against   vs.

Square No.   @

Page No.   Pg.

Diagram No.   D.

Denote No.   ()

Follow up with Black's move   _ _ _

Moves will be continued perpetually   _   _

_ _ _

13   THE DIFFERENCES BETWEEN "UNIVERSAL" CHESS AND CHINESE CHESS

(IN "UNIVERSAL" CHESS)

1. **STALEMATE**: is a draw.

2. **PERPETUAL CHECK**: is allowed to be played, and is a draw after the Threefold Repetition.

3. **CASTLING**: This special kind of movement involved the King and Rooks is allowed.

4. **CAPTURING EN PASSANT**: This Pawn to be captured in a passing movement is permitted.

5. **PAWN PROMOTION**: A Pawn can be promoted to be a Queen (or others) once he reaches the eighth/base rank.

6. **BOARD**: There are 64 squares arrayed in an 8x8 grid of alternately colored squares.

7. **SQUARES**: The board contains 64 squares. Each square is designated algebraic notations.

8. **PALACES AND BORDER (RIVER)**: None exist.

9. **THE PIECES**: There are a total of 32 pieces of chessmen, 16 on each side. Each White and Black side has: 1 King, 1 Queen, 2 Bishops, 2 Rooks, 2 Knights, and 8 Pawns.

10. **QUEENS**: One Queen on each side. The Queen, valued at 9, is the most powerful piece.

11. **KING**: The King moves one square at a time, in any direction, all over the board.

12. **BISHOPS**: One of the Bishops moves on white squares and one moves on black squares, they are valued at 3. They move diagonally and cannot leap over piece. The Bishop can only go to his squares of the same color.

13. **ROOKS**: Valued at 5, Rooks move horizontally or vertically and cannot leap over piece.

14. **KNIGHTS**: Knights valued at 3, can leap over one piece, friendly or unfriendly. The Knight moves in a form of an "L" shape and captures enemy pieces at the end-square of his move.

15. **PAWNS**: They can be promoted to Queen (or others), or have the ability to capture "En Passant" other pieces. The Pawns move one square at a time in any direction except backward. The first move of a Pawn has the option of advancing either one or two squares.

16. **PERPETUAL ATTACK**: is a legal move in "universal" CHESS. It is a drawn game if no changes occur after the Threefold Repetition of the perpetual attacks.

17. **CANNONS**: None exist.

13 THE DIFFERENCES BETWEEN "UNIVERSAL" CHESS AND CHINESE CHESS

(IN CHINESE CHESS OR "XIANGQI")

1. **STALEMATE**: is not a draw, but a mate.

2. **PERPETUAL CHECK**: is not allowed to be played, and it is not a draw but a forfeit.

3. **CASTLING**: No such movement in Chinese Chess.

4. **CAPTURING EN PASSANT**: None in Chinese Chess.

5. **PAWN PROMOTION**: A Pawn is always a Pawn, even if the Pawn reaches the bottom rank.

6. **THE BOARD**: There are nine files (nine vertical lines) numbering from 1 to 9, and ten ranks (ten horizontal lines) from 1 to 10. There are no shaded squares on Chinese Chessboard.

7. **SQUARES (INTERSECTIONS)**: There are ninety squares (in EZChess), or 90 intersections (in Chinese Chess) created from the Intersection of 9 Files and 10 Ranks, a difference from the 64 squares made up from 8 files and 8 ranks in CHESS.

8. **PALACES AND BORDER**: There is a border lines ("river" in Chinese Chess) in the middle of the board between the 5th and 6th ranks, and a palace on each side where the Kings and Queens are housed.

9. **THE PIECES**: There are a total of 32 pieces of chessmen in Chinese Chess, 16 on each side. Each White and Black side has: 1 King (General), 2 Queens (Counselors), 2 Bishops (Ministers in Red and Elephants in Black), 2 Rooks (Chariots), 2 Knights (Horses), 5 Pawns (Soldiers) and 2 Cannons (Cannons).

10. **QUEENS**: There are two Queens on each side. The Queens, valued at 1, are used primarily as the defensive or guard units. They move one square at a time diagonally within the palace.

11. **KING**: The Kings are prohibited to go out of the Palaces. The Kings can move forward, backward and sideways, not diagonally, one square at a time, and are subject to the Confrontation Rule, which is applied to the Kings only.

12. **BISHOPS**: The Bishops leap two squares diagonally at a time, and cannot cross over the Border. There is one Obstruction Rule which applies to the Bishops, that the Bishops cannot run over a piece, friendly or not. The Bishops are valued at 1.0.

13. **ROOKS**: Rooks move exactly like their counterparts in CHESS. The Rooks are valued at 5. They are the most powerful pieces in Chinese Chess.

14. **KNIGHTS**: Knights move exactly like their counterparts in CHESS, except there is an "Obstruction" Rule to restrict their movements in a certain ways. The Knights cannot jump over a piece, friendly or not, in the "long leg" of the "L-shape" movement. The Knights are valued at 2.5 points.

15. **PAWNS**: There is no "Promotion" to Queen (or others), nor "En Passant" other pieces for the Pawns. A Pawn is always a Pawn, and moves one square at a time, with no diagonal or backward movements. While the Pawns are still in their own territory, they can move forward only. Side movements for Pawns will be allowed only after crossing the border or "river".

16. **PERPETUAL ATTACK**: Perpetual attack is allowed and a legal move in CHESS. But in Chinese Chess, some perpetual attacks are legal and permissible, and some are not. (See "The Special Rules" in Chapter 6 in this book).

17. **CANNONS**: There are two (2) Cannons on each side and they are valued at 2.5. The Cannon must need a piece (but not more than one), friendly or not, in between the Cannon and its attacking target.

CHAPTER 2   ILLUSTRATIVE GAMES

1   ILLUSTRATIVE GAME NO.1

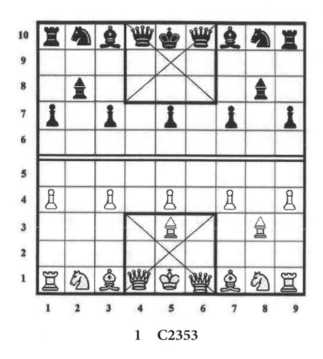

1   C2353

D 2.1.1.White starts the game by moving one of the Cannons to the center @53 in the 5th or King File. This Opening is called the "Center Cannon Opening". It is the most aggressive, effective and popular opening for White, in the past and in the present.

The Cannon @53 aiming for the Black King's Pawn @57 and the King's File, forces Black to find an effective ways to defend the Pawn and file.

For the convenience of our readers, the author prefers starting the opening moves of the game from left to right in this chapter. This is contradictory to the traditional Chinese customs (which is from right to left).

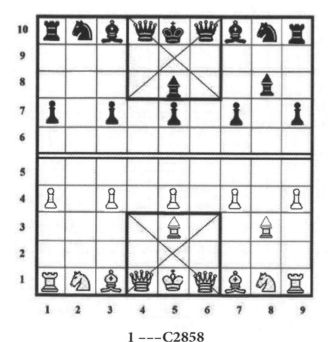

1 ---C2858

Black replies with the most aggressive and direct defense to the Center Cannon Opening, and he moves his Cannon to the center @58 as well, the same direction as the White Cannon.

With a Cannon at @58, Black can release most of the pressure from the center. Past plays have proved that, the White's next move of 2C5357+ is not considered good move, it'll merely help Black in developing his pieces faster.

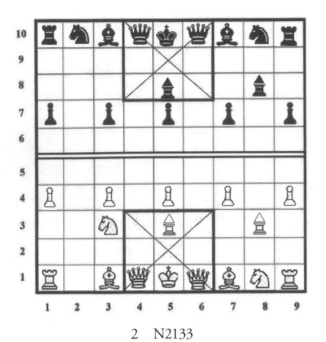

2   N2133

2.1.3. To develop the major pieces first is one of the most important rules of chess openings. Starting the Knight @33 from @21 has two purposes: to defend the vital King's Pawn and to make room for his Rook @11 to come out.

3   R1121

2.1.5. White moves his Rook out on the open file @21 as soon as possible, unlike the Rooks in CHESS games we normally play.

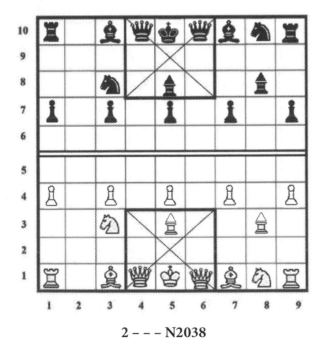

2 – – – N2038

2.1.4. Black follows one of the rudimentary principles of any opening: to bring out his Knight @38 as well.

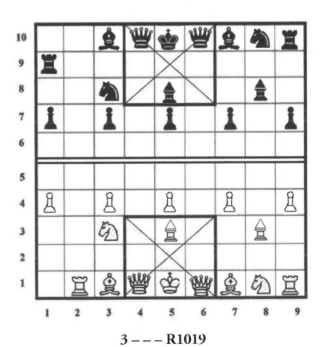

3 – – – R1019

2.1.6. Black follows the same aggressive pattern, another important Chinese Chess opening rule. He moves his Rook to @19 from @10.

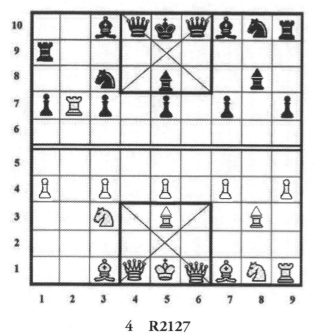

4   R2127

2.1.7. Moving the Rook to @27 is one of the many options open to White. Others options are R2125, N8173, P7475, P3435, etc.

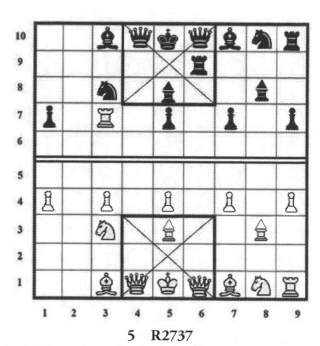

5   R2737

2.1.9. White continues by taking the Pawn @37 with his Rook, and, hence gives the Black Knight @38 some pressure. The Knight is defended by the Cannon @88.

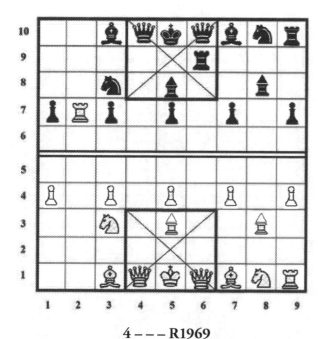

4 – – – R1969

2.1.8. Black follows his opening game plans by moving his Rook to @69. Other alternatives are: N8078, P3736, P7776, C8868, etc.

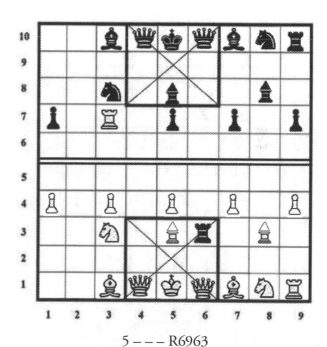

5 – – – R6963

2.1.10. The Black Rook @69 does not want to be idle and moves down @63 to attack the unprotected White Cannon @83, hoping the Cannon would go to @93, and the Knight @81 would be captured next by moving Rook to @83!

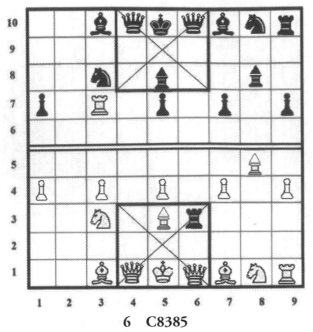

6   C8385

2.1.11. White of course will not fall into the trick. Instead, the Cannon @83 moves up to the Border @85, intending to move to @35 to help the Rook in attacking the Black Knight @ 38 and the Bishop @30

7   C8595

2.1.13. But surprising to Black, the White Cannon makes a strange move to @95, attacking the Black Rook @90, but also placing the Cannon itself into a self-trapped situation and a tempo losing move (forcing the Black Knight out to @98).

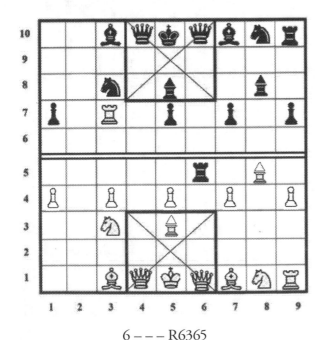

6 − − − R6365

2.1.12. Black has to retreat his Rook to @65 to stop the Cannon's move of C8535.

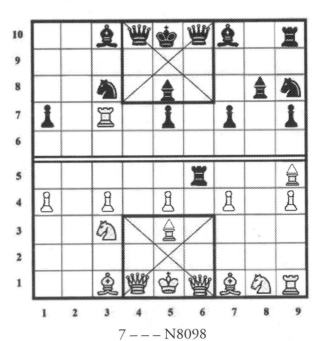

7 − − − N8098

2.1.14. Black has no better choice but to put his Knight to @98 from @80 to protect the Rook.

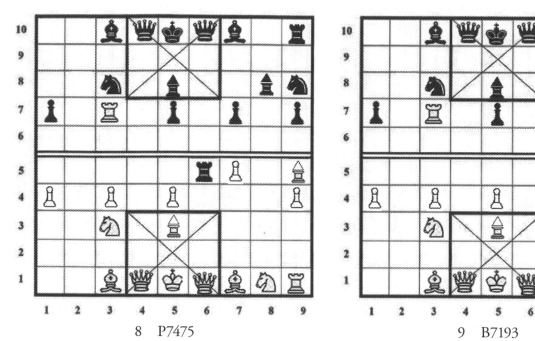

8   P7475

2.1.15. White moves his Pawn from @74 to @75, a very subtle move indeed. The Black Rook @65 is now under attack by the Cannon @95, should the innocent Pawn @75 be taken or not?

9   B7193

2.1.17. As planned, the White Bishop @71 is under attack by the Black Rook, moves to @93 to chase the Rook, hopefully out of the 5th Rank, so that the White Cannon @95 can move into @35.

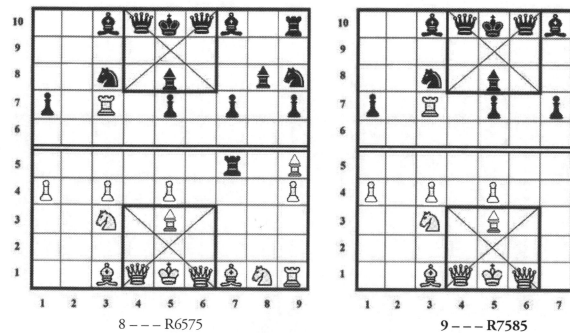

8 – – – R6575

2.1.16. The aggressive Black Rook @65 of course will not comply with the Cannon's wish by moving out of the 5th Rank. The Pawn is taken, a mistake! Black falls into a well-planned trap.

9 – – – R7585

2.1.18. Black Rook moves to @85, not only teaming up with the Cannon @88 to attack the White Knight @81, but trying to get rid of the troublesome Cannon @95 by moving his Pawn @97 to @96 next.

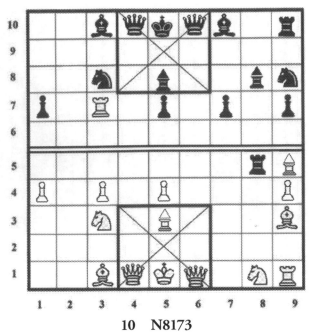

10   N8173

2.1.19. The Knight @81 is forced to come out to @73 naturally, and the Black Rook @85 is once again being chased.

11   R9181

2.1.21. Once the 8th File is cleared, White's second Rook is out @81, hunting the Black Cannon @88.

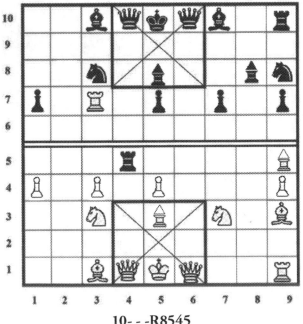

10- - -R8545

2.1.20. The overworked Black Rook is finally settled @45 and out of harm's way.

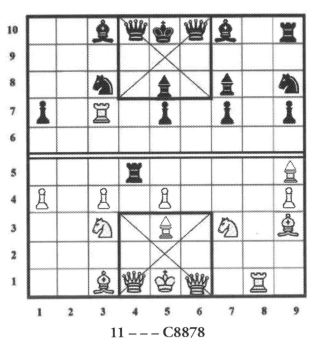

11 – – – C8878

2.1.22. The Black Cannon @88 side-steps the attack and moves to @78, attacking White's Knight @73.

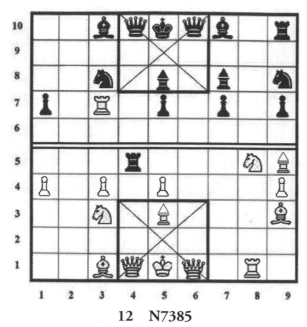

12   N7385

2.1.23. The White Knight @73 takes the opportunity to gain the tempo by moving up to @85, forcing the Black Rook out of the strategic 5th Rank finally. In the chess opening, gaining any tempo such as this is important.

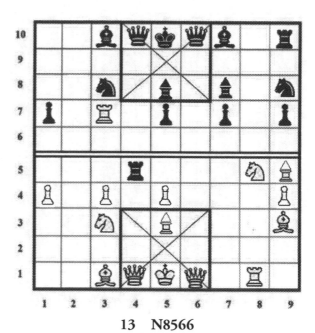

13   N8566

2.1.25. Instead of saving the Knight @33 from capture by the Black Rook, White employs a standard chess strategy called "To Gain on Exchange of Pieces", one of many chess mid-game strategies, by moving the Knight @85 to @66, to attack the hostile Cannon @78!. From the Diagram we can see White has his major offensive pieces in better positions, or in chess language, "Superior in mobility of pieces".

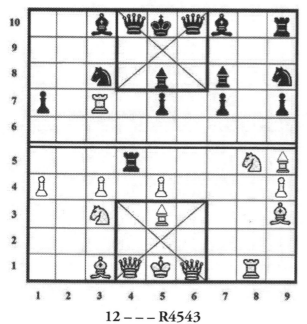

12 – – – R4543

2.1.24. The black Rook finds the unprotected Knight @33, and goes after it by moving to @43.

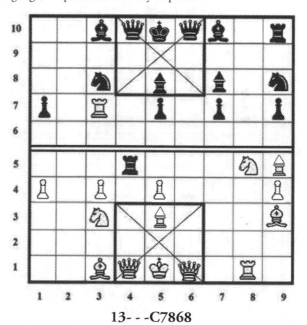

13- - -C7868

2.1.26. Not taking the Knight and moving the Cannon out of harm's way to @68 is the best defensive decision for Black. If 13..... R4333, 14 C9535! R3334, 15 N6678 N3819? 16 C5357+! Q6059, 17 C3530+ N1930, 18 R3730 next 19 R8189! Black would lose the Rook and the game. If 13.....R9080, 14 R8180 N9880, 15 N6678 N8078, 16 C9535 and White is still in highly advantageous position.

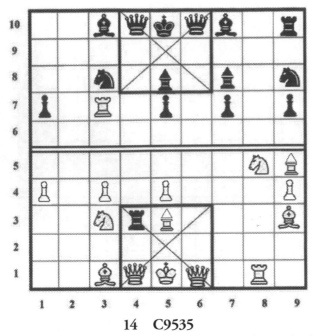

14 C9535

2.1.27. Black now is under heavy offensive pressure from White's Cannon @35.

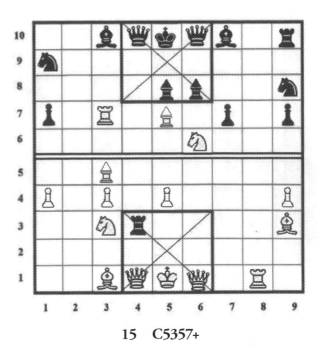

15 C5357+

2.1.29. Now, without protection of the Black Knight, the vital King's Pawn @57 becomes vulnerable and is immediately taken by the White's center Cannon!

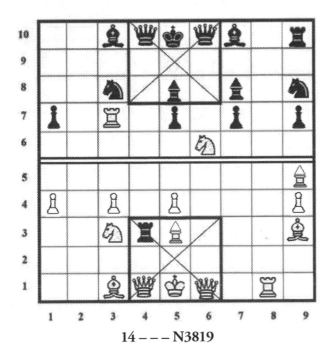

14 – – – N3819

2.1.28. Black's Knight @38 has no choice but to retreat to @19. The Cannon's protection from @68 is not enough.

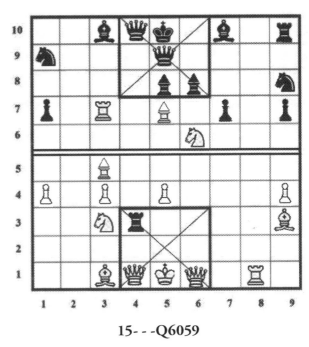

15- - -Q6059

2.1.30. The Black Queen @60 comes out to block the check from the Cannon @57.

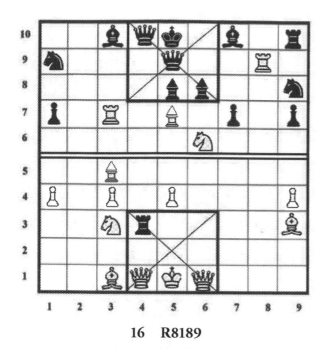

16   R8189

2.1.31. Now, with the Cannon in control @57, White moves his Rook down to @89, to carry out the mating task! In chess language, a mating net is laid down by White.

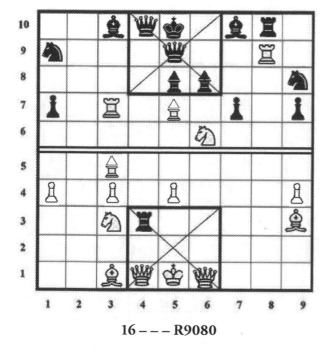

16 – – – R9080

2.1.32. Black realizes his forth coming troubles, and tries to exchange the killer Rook with the Rook out @80 but, it's too late!

17   R8969

2.1.33. The white Rook @89 surely declines the offer of a Rook exchange and moves to @69, planning the next move of N6678, next, a move of R6960 will be mate!

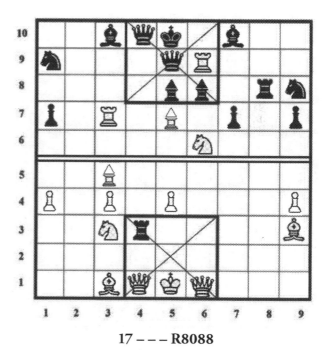

17 – – – R8088

2.1.34. Black Rook to @88 has two tasks: protect the Cannon @68 and, prevent the opponent Knight to @78.

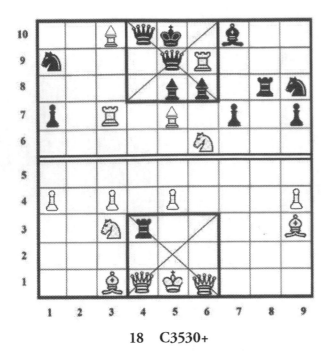

18   C3530+

2.1.35. White has another mating route, that is, the Cannon @35 makes a check by taking the Bishop @30.

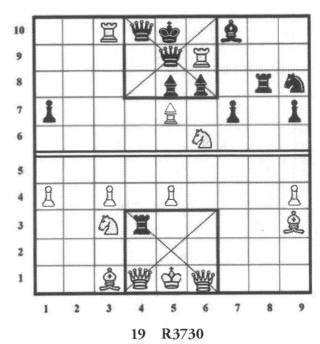

19   R3730

2.1.37. As planned, the White's Rook @37 takes the Knight and immediately threatens with R6959+ K5060, R5950+ K6069, a sure win for White next with R3039+! This is a typical chess mid-game mating situation (in chess language, a mating net): A combination of a few major pieces working on a kill with such perfect coordination and effectiveness.

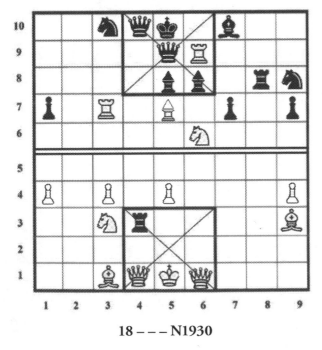

18 – – – N1930

2.1.36. The only answer to this check for Black is to capture the attacking Cannon @30 with the Knight from @19.

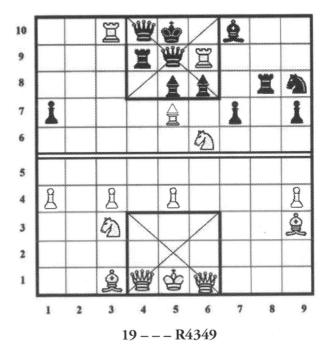

19 – – – R4349

2.1.38. The only solution for Black now is to bring down the Rook from @43 to @49 to guard the Queen @59.

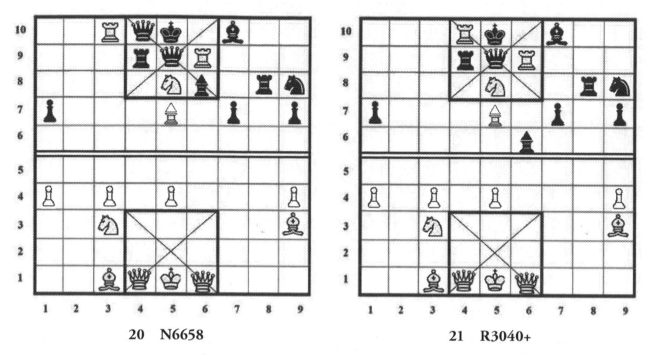

20 N6658

21 R3040+

2.1.39. With Black's persistent resistance, White has no choice but to take the Cannon @58 by the Knight @66. "Gain in Material (of pieces)" is another important strategy in chess mid-game play, an important factor in deciding a win.

2.1.41. But Rook's R3040+, a delightful and sneaky check, is a big shock to Black.

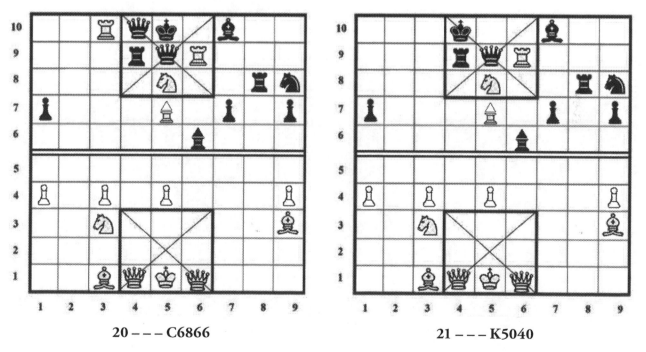

20 – – – C6866

21 – – – K5040

2.1.40. Black moves his Cannon @68 up to @66. Black hopes, the next move of C6665+ would capture the White Knight @65, and would possibly save the game. Or, if he is captured, the White Knight @58 could be taken by either the Rook @88 or Bishop @70.

2.1.42. There are two options: 1) Take away the Rook @40 by the King himself (as shown in

2.1.43. R6960+! What a crushing mating move by White! (Black Queen @59 is pinned by the Knight @58). Black resigns.

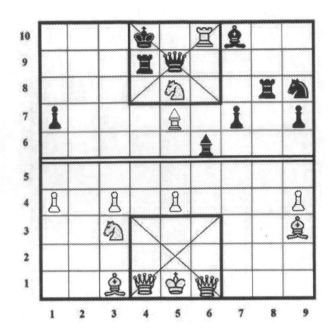

2 ILLUSTRATIVE GAME NO.2

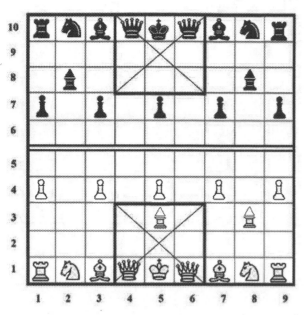

D2.2.1   1 C2353

White makes the most popular opening, the Center Cannon Opening, bring one of his Cannons to King's file @53, directly threatening to take the King's Pawn @57.

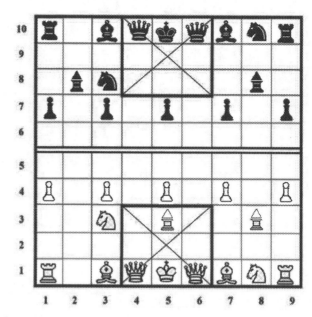

D2.2.3   2 N2133

White develops one of his major pieces, the Knight, with a move N2133, and makes room for the Rook @11 to come out fast.

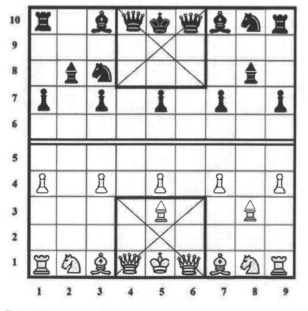

D2.2.2   1---N2038

Black answers with the effective Knight's Response by taking his Knight to @38 to protect the vital King's Pawn @57.

D2.2.4   2---P7776

Black chooses to move one of his Bishop Pawns to @76 to make room for the Knight @80 and the Rook @90 to develop later.

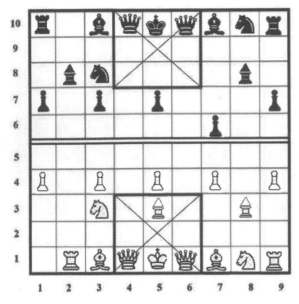

D2.2.5   3 R1121

Following one of the principles of opening, White develops one of his Rooks as early as possible by taking the R1121 move.

D2.2.7   4 R2125

White takes his Rook @21 up to the Border @25. This offense is popular lately, called Border Rook Offense. White's intention is to offer a Pawn exchange @75 and Rook can take over @75, making room for White Knight @81 to develop.

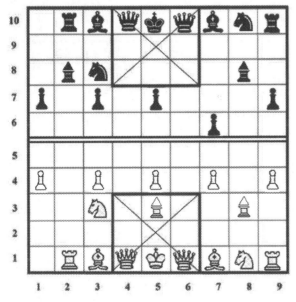

D2.2.6   3---R1020

Black does the same thing, by developing the Rook @10 out with the move R1020, to back up the Cannon @28.

D2.2.8   4--- N8078

Black brings another Knight to protect the King's Pawn @57. The defensive opening with the two Black knights located @38 and @78 respectively to protect the King's Pawn, is named by the author the "Double-Knights Defense", the most popular defense against the Center Cannon Opening.

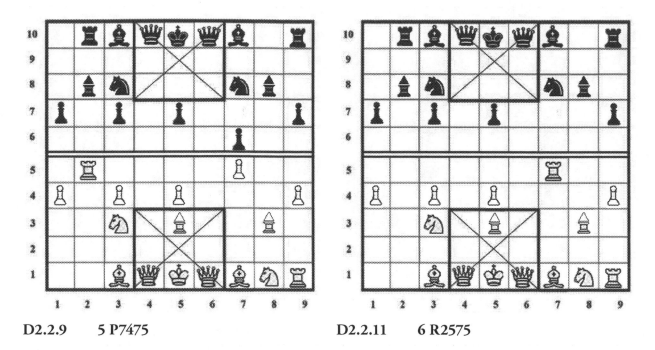

D2.2.9   **5 P7475**

White offers a Pawn exchange with P7475 as planned. Black can either accept the exchange or bring one of the Bishops to @58.

D2.2.11   **6 R2575**

The White Rook occupies @75 as planned. The Black Knight @78 is under some pressure from the White Rook @75.

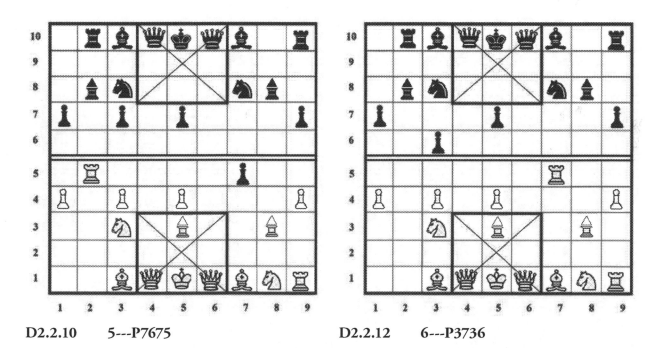

D2.2.10   **5---P7675**

Black accepts the exchange.

D2.2.12   **6---P3736**

Black moves the other Bishop Pawn to @36. The better move could be 6---C8889, next move 7--C8979! White would be under pressure.

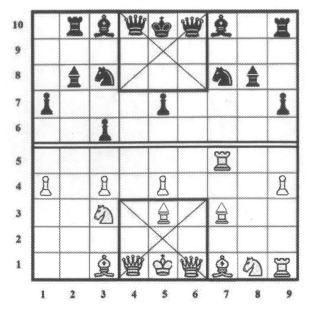

D2.2.13   7 C8373

Instead of developing the Knight @81, White develops his Cannon @83 to @73 to attack the Black Knight @78, forcing the Knight to run.

D2.2.15   8 R7576

White, unaware of danger, moves to @76, hoping to force the Knight to retreat back to @98, the only square the Knight can escape to. And the Cannon can start an offense with a move C7370+.

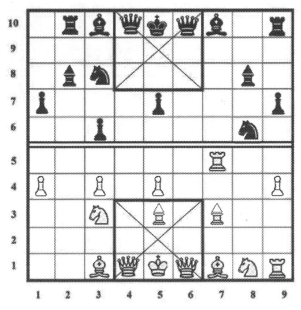

D2.2.14   7---N7886

After evaluation, Black turns a crisis into an opportunity in this midgame phase. He sets up a subtle trap for the White Rook, by moving the Knight up to @86 to entice the Rook into @76.

D2.2.16   8---C2826

To White's surprise, Black makes a well-planned attack on the Rook with C2826! It looks like a mistake, because Black's two Knights @38 and @86 would be under attack simultaneously by the White Rook @36.

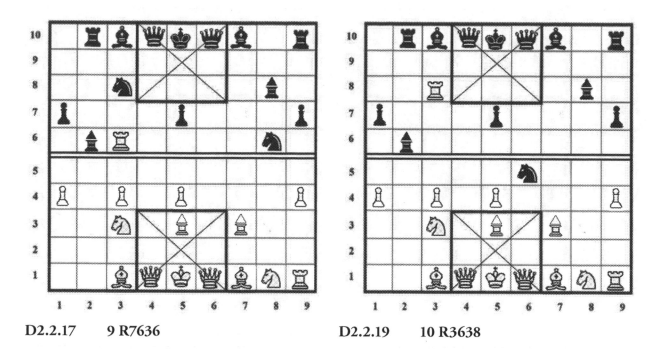

D2.2.17   9 R7636

White Rook takes the Pawn @36, a greedy mistake. White neglects a few principles of midgame plays: 1. the purpose of Black's move, 2. evaluation of that particular situations, and lastly, underestimates his opponent.

D2.2.19   10 R3638

White makes another fatal mistake. He accepts the gambit and takes the Knight @38.

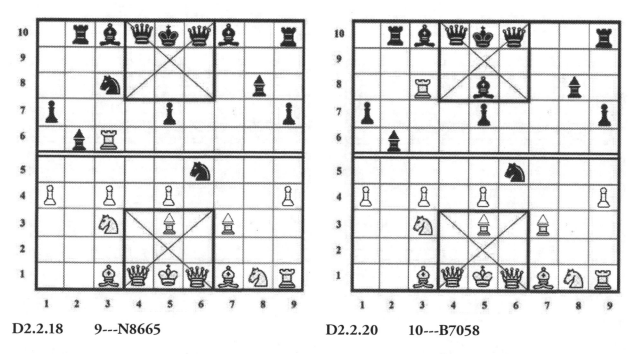

D2.2.18   9---N8665

Another surprise move, Black sacrifices his Knight @38, and moves the other Knight to @65. It is obviously a part of Black's counterattack plan.

D2.2.20   10---B7058

Black moves the Bishop B7058 to force the Rook to run, also opens the room for Black Rook @90 to come out to enforce the counter-attack.

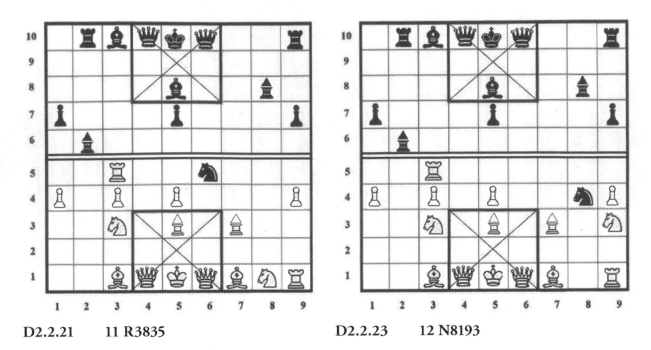

D2.2.21   11 R3835

White Rook is now under fire from the Black Cannon @88, and has to retreat back to the square @35, to help to solidify his defense.

D2.2.23   12 N8193

White has no better choice but to make the Knight @81 to @93 to protect the square @72. This does not prevent the Knight @24 from making a check.

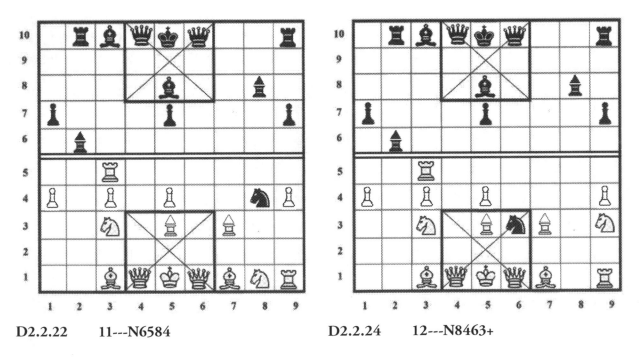

D2.2.22   11---N6584

After Black solidifies his defense by connecting the Bishops, now Black initiates his Knight @65 to start the attack after the move of N6584! The next move of N8472+ will fork the King and the Rook @91.

D2.2.24   12---N8463+

The square @72 is protected, so the Black Knight makes a check with the move of N8463+, and Black draws the first blood.

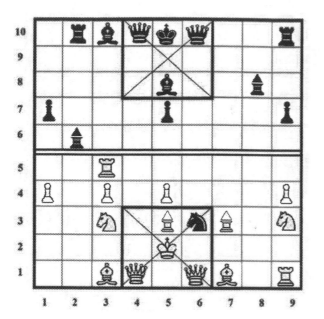

D2.2.25   13 K5152

White King has to move to square @52 to escape the check from the Knight @63.

D2.2.27   14 K5242

In order to escape the checkmate from the enemy Rook, the White King must move to @42. Moving the Cannon @53 out of the way to make room for the King is impossible: If 14 C5343 R2022+, 15 K5253 C6656+, 16 R3555 N6355 (A White Rook is lost and so will be the game).

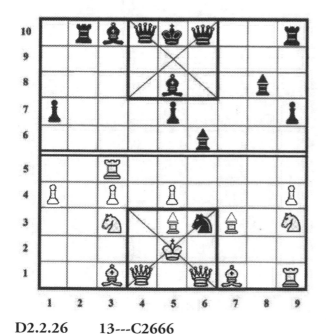

D2.2.26   13---C2666

Black Cannon @26 gets out of the 2nd file with a move of C2666, opens the file for the Rook @20 to make the checkmate.

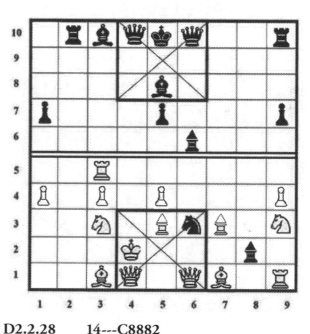

D2.2.28   14---C8882

Black plays the Cannon wisely from @88 to @82, instead of placing Rook to @70 to attack the White Cannon @73. It serves two purposes: 1. to prevent White to play his Queens to @52, and 2. to block White Rook @91 from coming out.

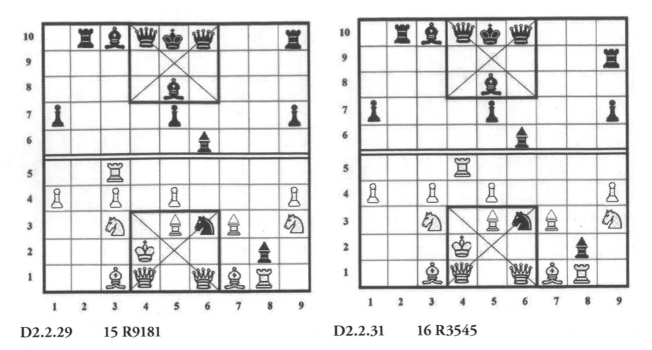

D2.2.29   15 R9181

Anyhow the White Rook finally comes out, but, it is too late to turn the tide.

D2.2.31   16 R3545

Seeing the Black Rook @99 will move to 4th file for a check, the White Rook @35 takes control of the file first by a move of R3545.

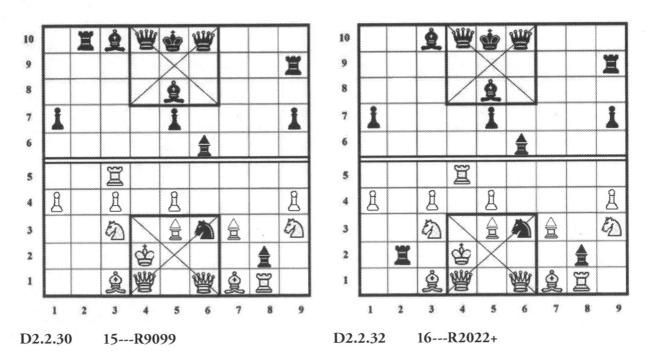

D2.2.30   15---R9099

Black's Cannon @82 appears in danger but it is safe. The Rook @20 is indirectly protecting him. It is Black's time to finish the job by bringing out the other Rook to provide the final strike.

D2.2.32   16---R2022+

White takes the strike with the filed Rook from @20 to @22.

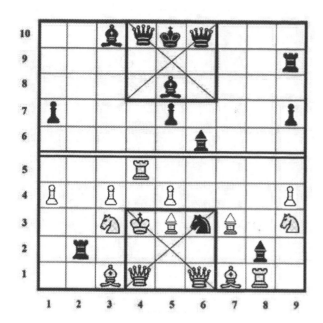

D2.2.33   17 K4243

The White King has no other route to escape except to @43.

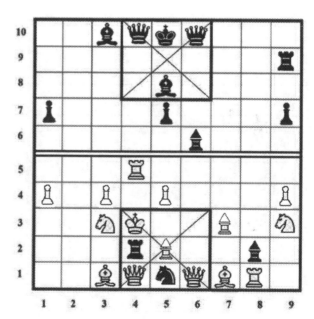

D2.2.35   18 C5352

White puts the Cannon reluctantly from @53 to @52 to block the Knight's check, and makes a square @53 for the King to escape from mate.

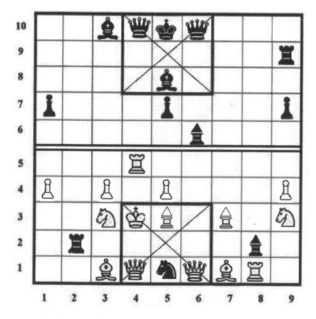

D2.2.34   17---N6351+

The Black Knight again makes an unorthodox move of N6351 checking the King! White cannot play his Queens to obstruct the Knight from checking, because a mate will be made with R2242!

D2.2.36   18---R2242+

The inevitable strike comes with Rook making the check move of R2242.

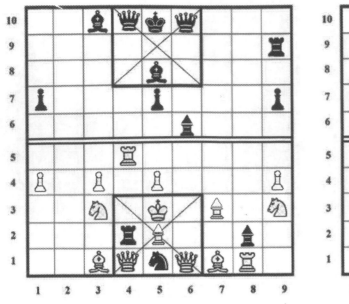

D2.2.37   19 K4353

The White King moves to @53 and leaves his Rook @45 to be captured.

D2.2.39   20 R8182

The last thing White can do now is to get the surviving Rook out by taking the annoying Cannon @82, with a move of R8182.

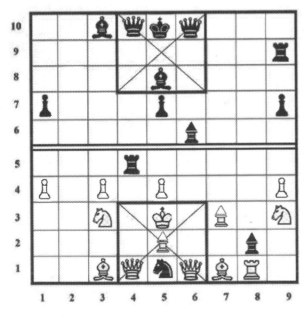

D2.2.38   19---R4245

The White Rook @45 is captured by the Black Rook.

D2.2.40   20---C6656+

Black gives White no chance of any counter-attack and finishes the mating with one- two punch: (The first punch with a Cannon move of C6656+).

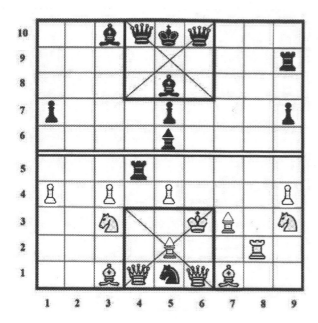

D2.2.41   21 K5363

The white King unwillingly runs to @63 to escape from the attack. This move will be his final move. Either one of the two Black Rooks can make the checkmate.

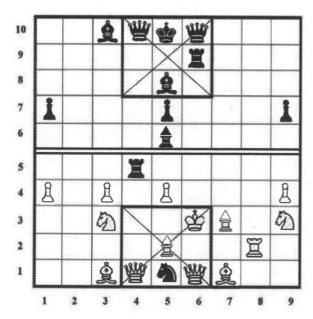

D2.2.42   21---R9969#

Black prefers the Rook from somewhere out of the blue to do the job and wins the game. And White resigns.

CHAPTER 3   SOME BASIC CHECKMATES

1.   PAWN

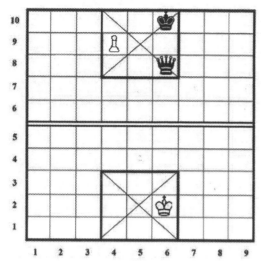

D 3.1.1
1 P4959 #

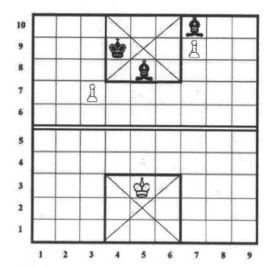

D 3.1.3
1	P7969	B7098
2	P3747	B9876
3	K5343	B7698
4	P4748+	K4940
5	P4849+	K4050
6	P4940#	

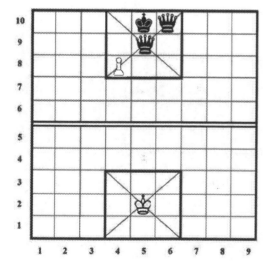

D 3.1.2
1 P4849#

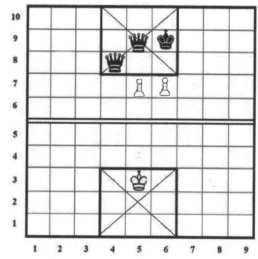

D 3.1.4
1	P5758	K6960
2	P6757	K6069
3	P5747	K6960
4	P4748	Q5948
5	P5848	K6069
6	P4858	K6960
7	P5859#	

2. KNIGHT

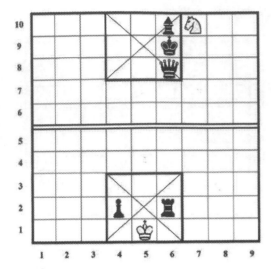

D 3.2.1
1 N7880#

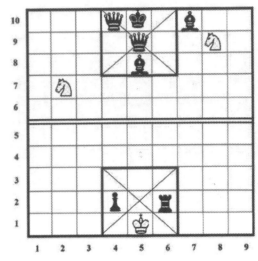

D 3.2.3
1 N2739#

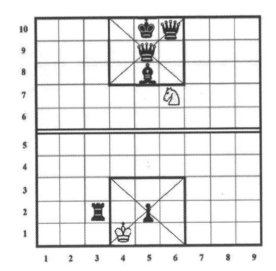

D 3.2.2
1 N6779#

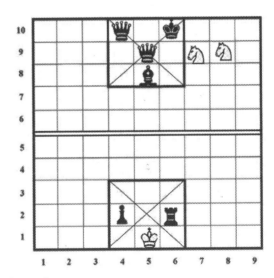

D 3.2.4
1   N7958+   K6050
2   N5839#
OR
1   N7958+   K6069
2   N5877#

3.   KNIGHT AND PAWN

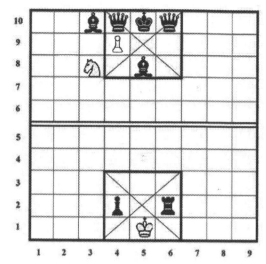

D 3.3.1

1 P4940#

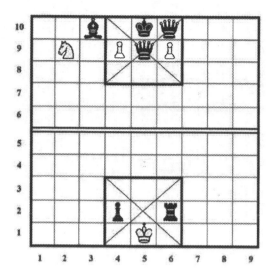

D 3.3.3

1   P4940+   Q5940

2   N2948#

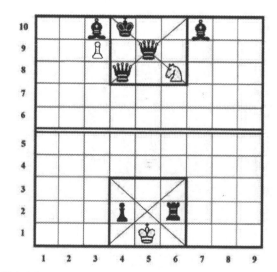

D 3.3.2

1 P3930#

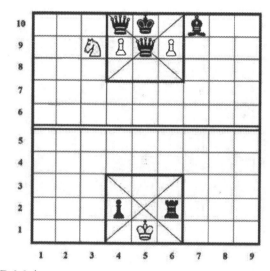

D 3.3.4

1 P4959#

4. CANNON

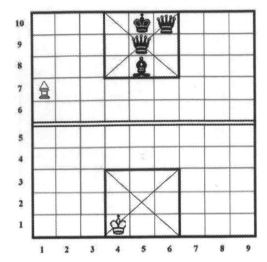

D 3.4.1
1 C1757#

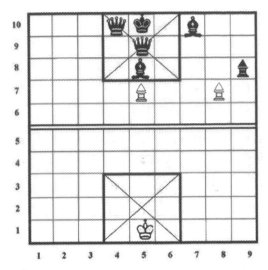

D 3.4.3
1 C8780#

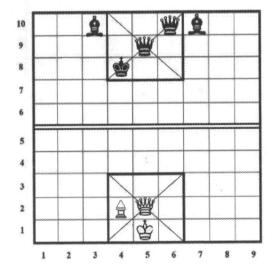

D 3.4.2
1 Q5243#

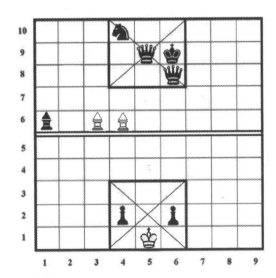

D 3.4.4
1 C4649+   K6960
2 C3630+   N4069
3 C4940#
OR
1 C4649+   Q5948
2 C3666#

5. CANNON AND PAWN

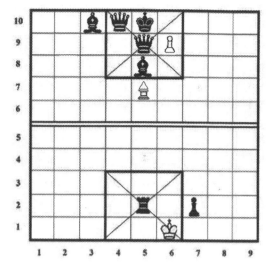

D 3.5.1
1 P6960#

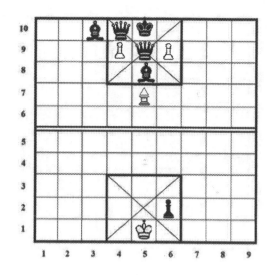

D 3.5.3

1	K5141	P6252
2	P4940#	

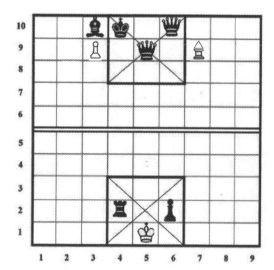

D 3.5.2
1 C7970#

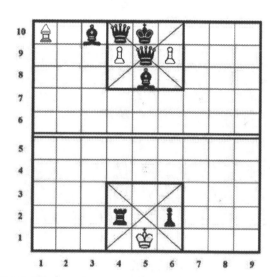

D 3.5.4
1 P4959#

6.   KNIGHT AND CANNON

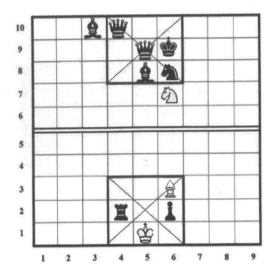

D 3.6.1
1 N6788#

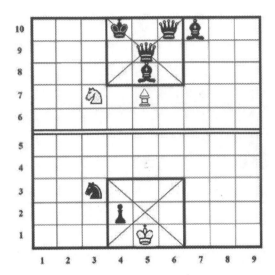

D 3.6.3

1	N3729+	K4049
2	C5717	P4252+
3	K5161	N3354
4	1719#	

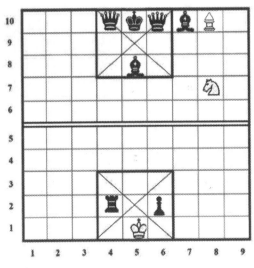

D 3.6.2

1	N8779+	K5059
2	C8089#	

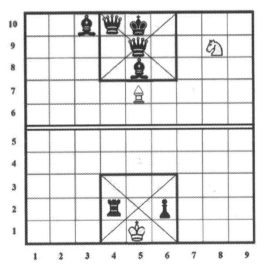

D 3.6.4

1	N8968+	K5060
2	C5767#	

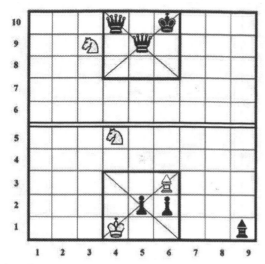

D 3.6.5

1	N4566+	Q5968
2	N6678#	

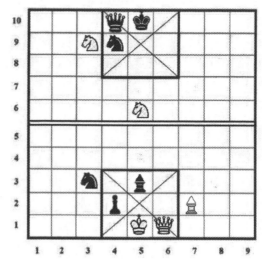

D 3.6.7

1	N5668+	K5059
2	N3947+	K5969
3	C7262+	C5363
4	N6849+	C6353
5	N4968+	C5363
6	N6889+	C6353
7	N4768+	C5363
8	N8977+	K6960
9	N6849#	

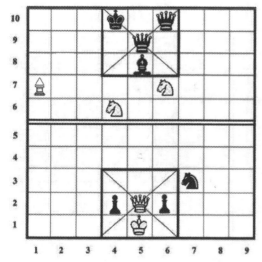

D 3.6.6

1	N4638+	K4049
2	N3820+	K4940
3	C1710+	B5830
4	N2038+	K4049
5	N3857+	K4948
6	N5745+	K4858
7	N4537+	K5868
8	N3756+	K6869
9	N6788#	

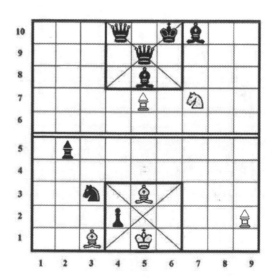

D 3.6.8

1	N7789+	K6050
2	C9290#	

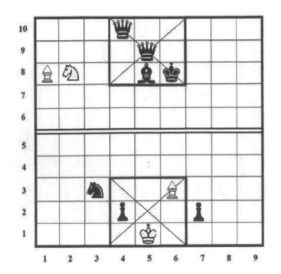

D 3.6.9
1   N2847+   K6869
2   N4768#

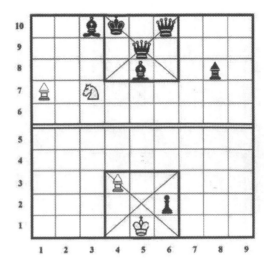

D 3.6.11
1   C1710   B3018
2   N3729+   K4050
3   N4340+   B5830
4   C4049#

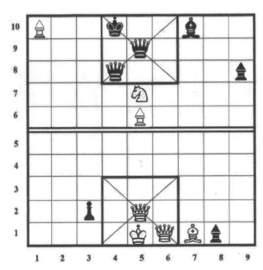

D 3.6.10
1   N5749   B7058
2   N4920+   B5830
3   N2038+   K4049
4   C5646#

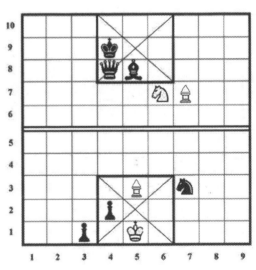

D 3.6.12
1   C5343+   Q4859
2   N6748+   K4948
3   C7747#

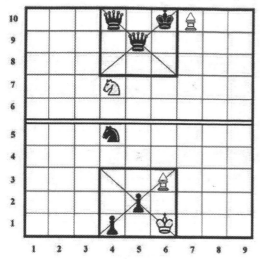

D 3.6.13

1	N4768+	N4566
2	N6889+	K6050
3	N8960#	

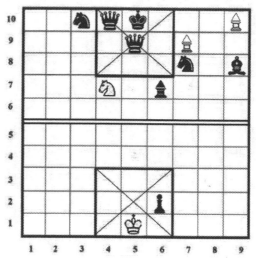

D 3.6.15

1	C7970+	N7880
2	N4768+	K5060
3	N6889+	K6050
4	C7078+	N8069
5	C9060	P6261+
6	K5152	C6760
7	C7870#	

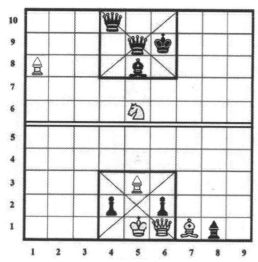

D 3.6.14

1	N5677+	K6960
2	C1810+	B5830
3	N7789+	K6069
4	C1019+	Q5948
5	C5359#	

7. KNIGHT, CANNON AND PAWN

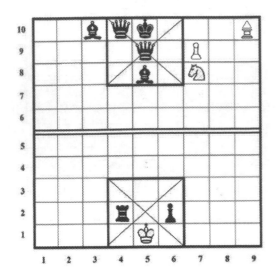

D 3.7.1

1	P7970+	Q5960
2	P7060#	

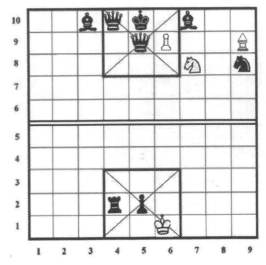

D 3.7.3

1	C9990+	N9880
2	P6960+	Q5960
3	C9070+	Q6059
4	N7860#	

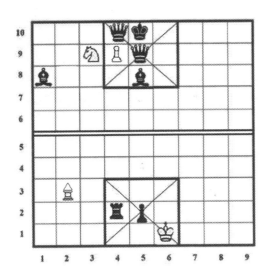

D 3.7.2

1	C2320+	B1830
2	P4959+	K5059
3	C2029#	

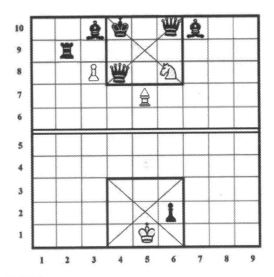

D 3.7.4

1	C5747+	Q4859
2	P3848+	R2949
3	P4849#	

8. ROOK

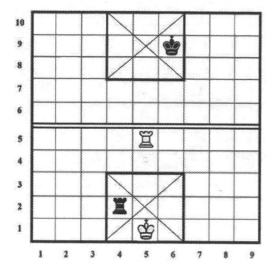

D 3.8.1
1 R5565#

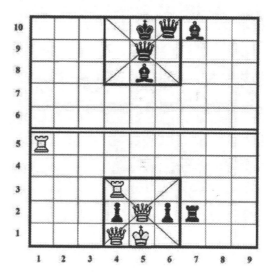

D 3.8.3

1	R1510+	B5830
2	R1030+	Q5940
3	R3040+	K5059
4	R4049+	K5950
5	R4353+	Q6059
6	R5359+	K5060
7	R4940#	

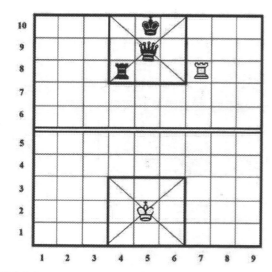

D 3.8.2
1 R7870#

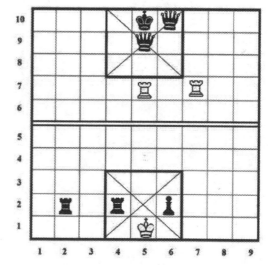

D 3.8.4

1	R5759+	Q6059
2	R7770#	

OR

1	R5759+	K5040
2	R5950+	K4049
3	R7779+	K4948
4	R5040#	

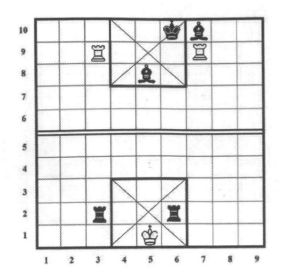

D 3.8.5
1   R3969+   R6469
2   R7970#

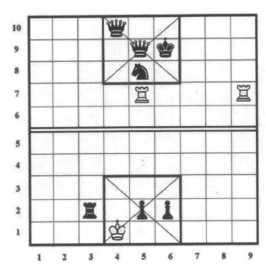

D 3.8.7
1   R9767+   Q5968
2   R6768+   K6968
3   R5767#
OR
1   R9767+   Q5968
2   R6768+   K6959
3   R5758#

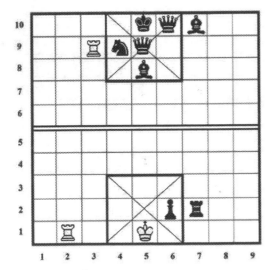

D 3.8.6
1   R2120+   Q5940
2   R2040+   K5040
3   R3930#

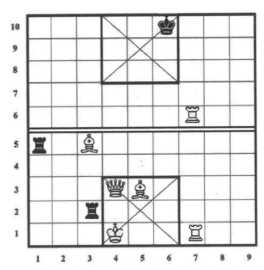

D 3.8.8
1   R7666+   K6050
2   R7151   R1511+
3   B5331+   K5040
4   R6646#

9.   ROOK AND PAWN

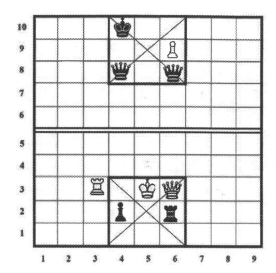

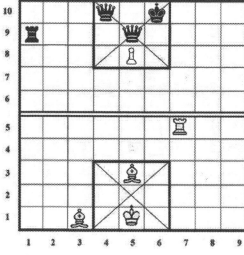

D 3.9.1

1	R3330+	K4049
2	R3039+	K4940
3	P6960	Q6859
4	P6050+	K4050
5	R3930#	

D 3.9.3

1	P5868	K6050
2	P6869	Q5960
3	P6960+	K5060
4	R7570+	K6069
5	R7079+	K6960
6	R7919>>	

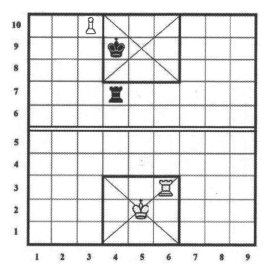

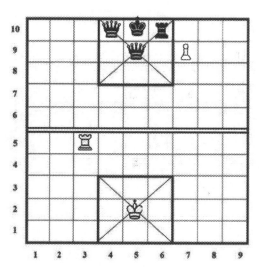

D 3.9.2

1	R6353	R4742+
2	K5251	R4241+
3	K5152	R4147
4	R5350	R4737
5	R5040#	

D 3.9.4

1	R3585	R6068
2	R8580+	R6860
3	R8070	R6070
4	P7970#	

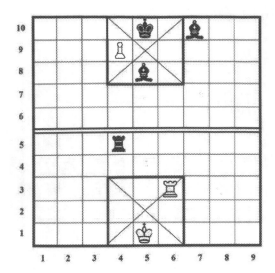

D 3.9.5

1	K5161	R4549
2	R6360+	K5059
3	R6069+	K5950
4	R6949>>	

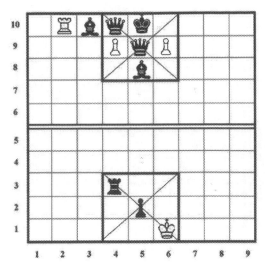

D 3.9.7

1	P6959+	Q4059
2	R2030+	Q5940
3	R3040#	

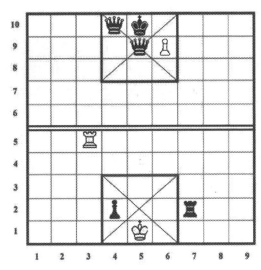

D 3.9.6

1	P6959+	Q4059
2	R3530#	

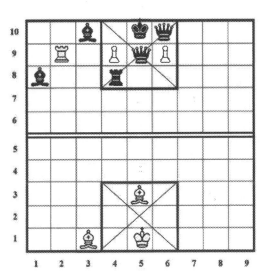

D 3.9.8

1	P4959+	Q6059
2	R2959+	K5040
3	P6960	R4858
4	P6050#	

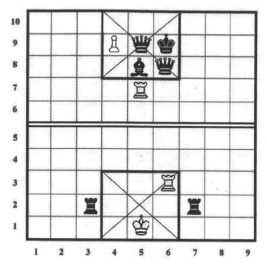

D 3.9.9

1	P4959+	K6959
2	R5758+	K5969
3	R6368#	

D 3.9.11

1	R2320+	B5830
2	R2030+	Q5940
3	R3040+	K5059
4	R4049+	K5958
5	R4948+	K5859
6	R4849+	K5958
7	R1518#	

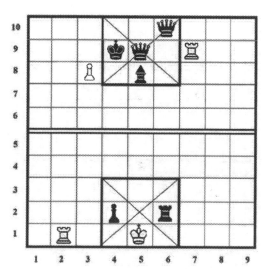

D 3.9.10

1	R2129+	K4940
2	R2920+	K4049
3	P3839+	K4948
4	R2040+	Q5940
5	R7949#	

D 3.9.12

1	P3949+	K4049
2	R3646+	Q5948
3	R4648+	K4948
4	R3747#	

OR

1	P3949+	R2949
2	R3730+	R2030
3	R3630#	

10. ROOK AND KNIGHT

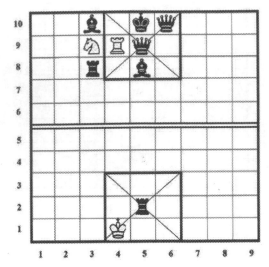

D 3.10.1
1 R4940#

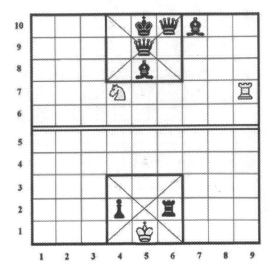

D 3.10.3
1	N4739+	K5040
2	R9747+	Q5948
3	R4748#	

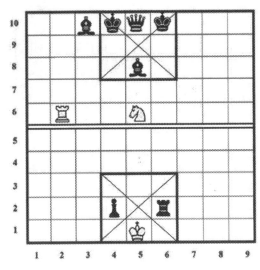

D 3.10.2
1	N5648+	K5059
2	R2629#	

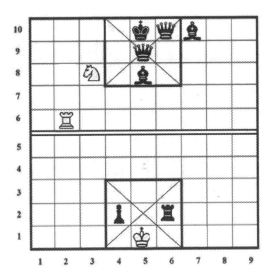

D 3.10.4
1	R2620+	Q5940
2	R2040#	

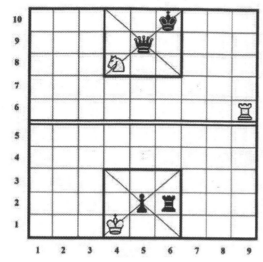

D 3.10.5
1 R9690#

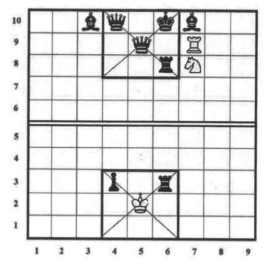

D 3.10.7
1	R7970+	K6069
2	R7060+	Q5960
3	N7880#	

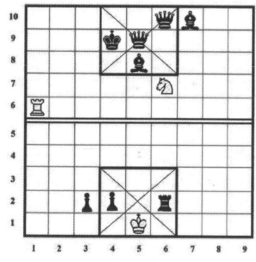

D 3.10.6
| 1 | R1646+ | Q5948 |
| 2 | R4648# | |

D 3.10.8
1	R7870+	K6968
2	R7078+	K6869
3	R7888+	K6960
4	R8880#	

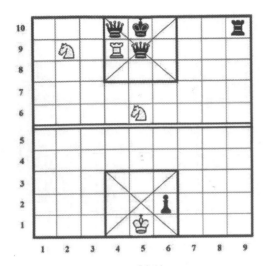

D 3.10.9

1	N5668+	K5060
2	N6889+	K6069
3	N2948#	

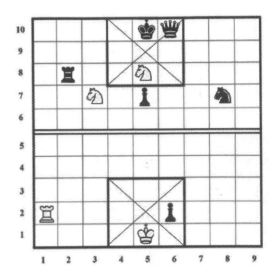

D 3.10.11

1	R1210+	K5059
2	R1019+	K5950
3	N5839+	K5059
4	N3947+	K5958
5	N4755+	K5868
6	N5576#	

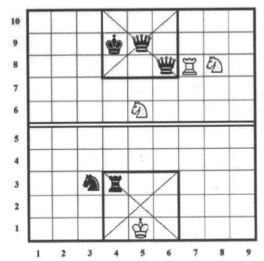

D 3.10.10

1	N5637+	K4948
2	R7868+	Q5968
3	N8867#	

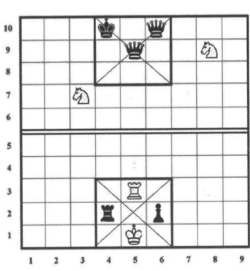

D 3.10.12

1	N3729+	K4049
2	N8960+	Q5960
3	N2937+	K4940
4	R5350#	

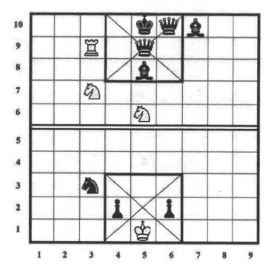

D 3.10.13
1   R3930+   B5830
2   N5668+   K5040
3   N3729#

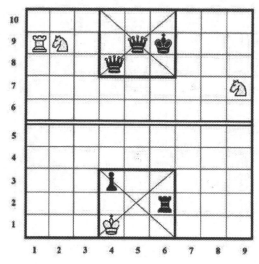

D 3.10.15
1   N2948+   K6968
2   N4856+   K6858
3   N5637+   K5868
4   N9789+   K6869
5   N8977+   K6968
6   N3756#

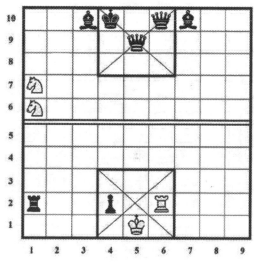

D 3.10.14
1   R6260+   Q5960
2   N1729+   K4049
3   N1637#

D 3.10.16
1   R7370+   B5870
2   N8768+   K5060
3   N6889+   K6050
4   N9879+   K5060
5   N7958+   K6050
6   N5879+   K5060
7   N7967+   K6050
8   N7648#

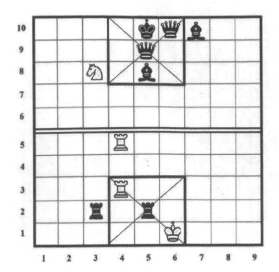

D 3.10.17
| 1 | R4540+ | Q5940 |
| 2 | R4340# | |

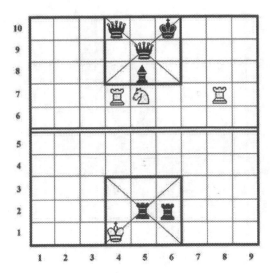

D 3.10.19
1	R4740+	Q5940
2	R8780+	K6069
3	R8089+	K6960
4	N5778+	K6050
5	R8980+	K6260
6	R8060#	

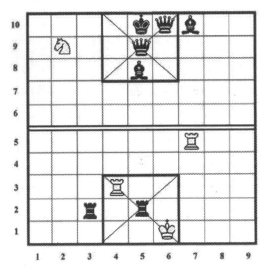

D 3.10.18
1	R4340+	Q5940
2	N2948+	K5059
3	R7579#	

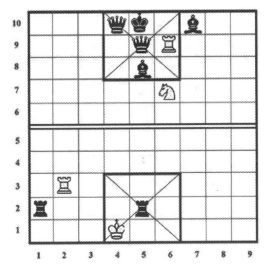

D 3.10.20
1	R6959+	K5060
2	R5950+	K6050
3	N6748+	K5059
4	R2329#	

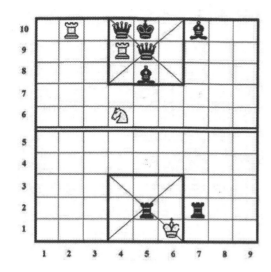

D 3.10.21

1	R4959+	K5059
2	N4638+	K5949
3	R2040#	

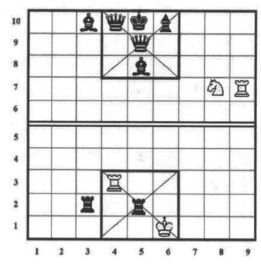

D 3.10.23

1	N8779+	C6069
2	R9790+	Q5960
3	R9060+	K5059
4	R6069+	K5950
5	R6949#	

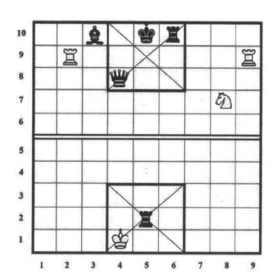

D 3.10.22

1	N8779+	K5040
2	R2949+	K4049
3	N7958#	

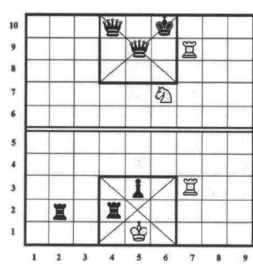

D 3.10.24

1	R7970+	K6069
2	N6788+	K6968
3	R7378+	K6869
4	R7858#	

11. ROOK, KNIGHT AND PAWN

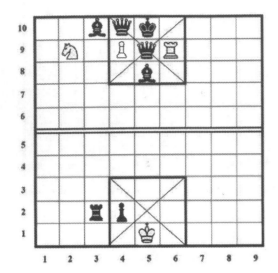

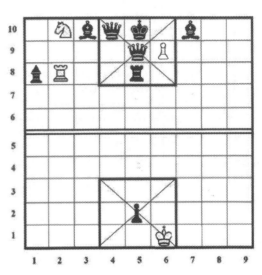

D 3.11.1

1	P4940+	Q5940
2	N2948#	

D 3.11.3

1	R2858	B3058
2	N2018	Q5968
3	N1839#	

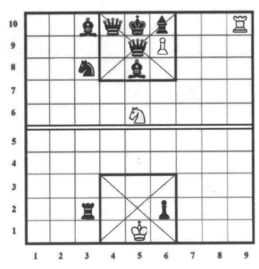

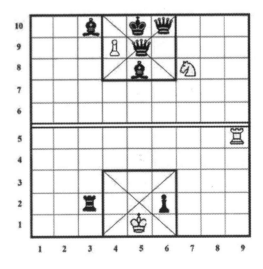

D 3.11.2

1	R9060+	Q5960
2	N5648#	

OR

1	N5658+	Q5948,
2	R9060#	

D 3.11.4

1	P4959+	Q6059
2	R9590+	Q5960
3	R9060#	

OR

1	P4959+	K5040
2	R9545#	

12. ROOK AND CANNON

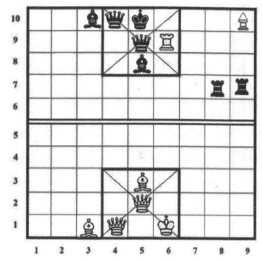

D 3.12.1
1 R6960#

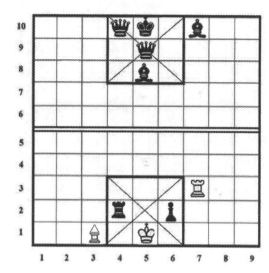

D 3.12.3
1	C3130+	B5830
2	R7370#	

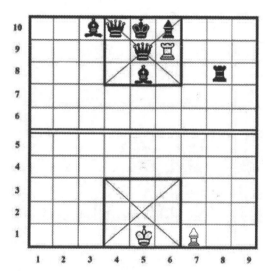

D 3.12.2
1 C7170#

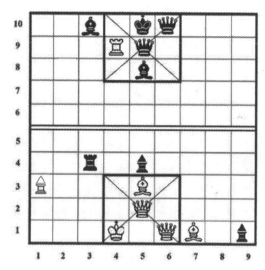

D 3.12.4
1	C1310+	Q5940
2	R4940+	K5059
3	R4049#	

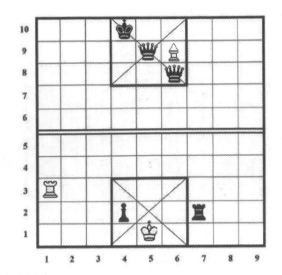

D 3.12.5
1 R1310#

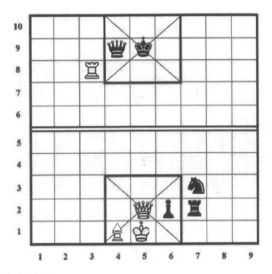

D 3.12.7
1   R3848+   K4948
2   Q5243#

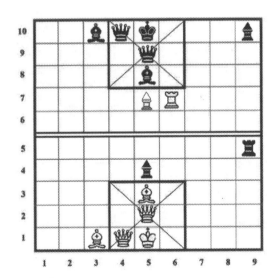

D 3.12.6
1   K5161   R9591+
2   K6162   C5464
3   R6764   C9060+
4   R6460#

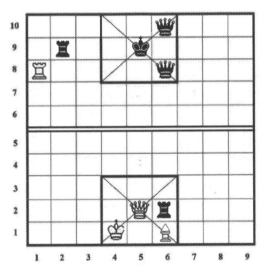

D 3.12.8
1   R1858+   K5969
2   R5868+   K6959
3   C6151#

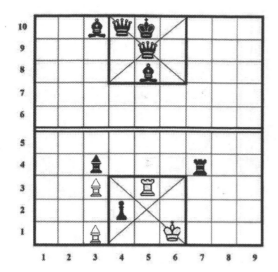

D 3.12.9

1	C3330+	B5830
2	C3130#	

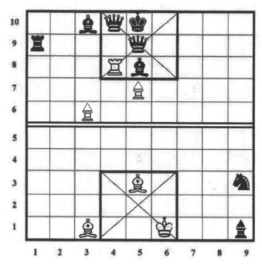

D 3.12.11

1	R4838	N9381+
2	B5371	N8173+
3	K6162	N7354+
4	B3153	R1912+
5	K6263	B3018
6	R3818	R1232
7	C3656	N5466
8	R1858	N6658
9	C5658#	

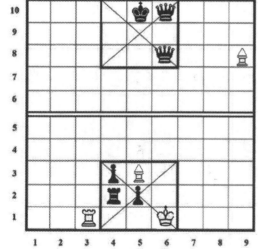

D 3.12.10

1	R3130+	K5059
2	R3039+	K5950
3	C9890#	

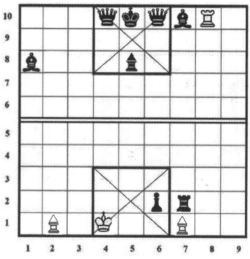

D 3.12.12

1	C2120+	B1830
2	C7170+	Q6059
3	C7040+	Q5960
4	C4060+	B3018
5	C6068+	K5059
6	R8089+	K5950
7	C6818	P6252
8	C1810#	

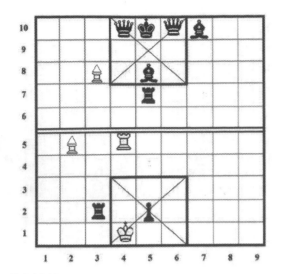

D 3.12.13
1	C2520+	B5830
2	R4540+	K5059
3	R4049+	K5958
4	C2028#	

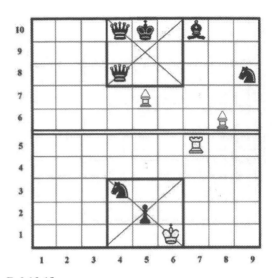

D 3.12.15
1	R7570+	K5059
2	R7050+	K5949
3	C5747+	Q4859
4	C8646#	

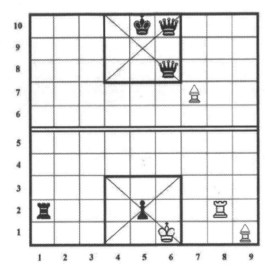

D 3.12.14
1	C9190+	K5059
2	R8289+	K5958
3	C9098+	Q6859
4	C7778#	

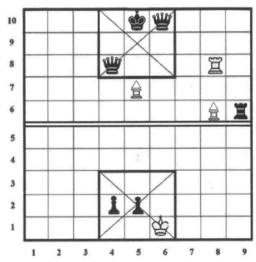

D 3.12.16
1	R8858+	K5040
2	C5747+	Q4859
3	R5848+	K4050
4	C8680#	

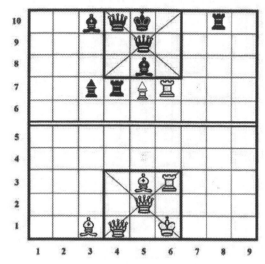

D 3.12.17
1   R6760+   R8060
2   R6360#

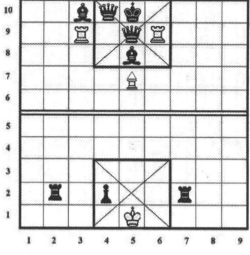

D 3.12.19
1   R6959+   Q4059
2   R3930#
OR
1   R6959+   K5060
2   R5950#

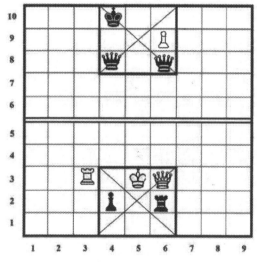

D 3.12.18
1   R4959+   R7959
2   R9060#

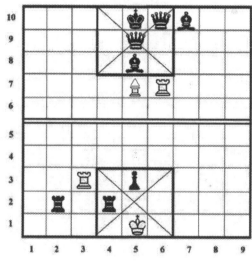

D 3.12.20
1   R3330+   R4240
2   K5161   R2221+
3   K6162   R2122+
4   K6261   R4030
5   R6760#

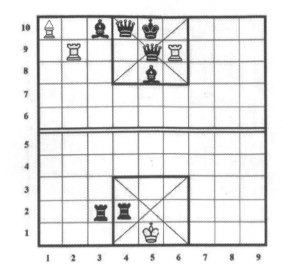

D 3.12.21
1 R2959#

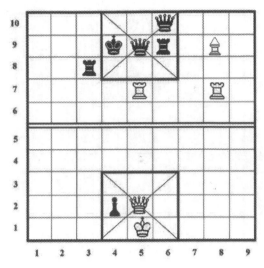

D 3.12.23

1	R5747+	R3848
2	R4748+	K4948
3	Q5243	K4849
4	R8747#	

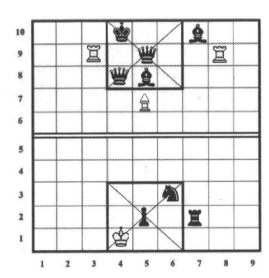

D 3.12.22

1	R3949+	K4050
2	R8959+	Q4859
3	R4940#	

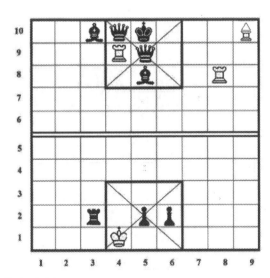

D 3.12.24

1	R8880+	B5870
2	R8070+	Q5960
3	R4940+	K5059
4	R7079+	K5958
5	R4048#	

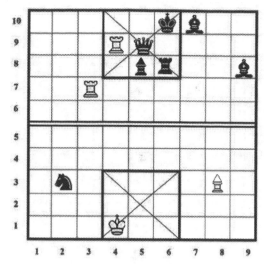

D 3.12.25

1	C8380+	K6069
2	R4959+	K6959
3	R3739#	

D 3.12.27

1	R1610+	Q5940
2	R1040+	N3840
3	C3130#	

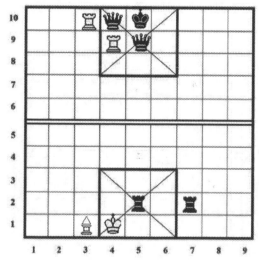

D 3.12.26

1	R3040+	Q5940
2	C3130+	Q4059
3	R4940#	

D 3.12.28

1	R4959+	K5059
2	R8789+	K5950
3	C9790#	

13.   ROOK, CANNON AND PAWN

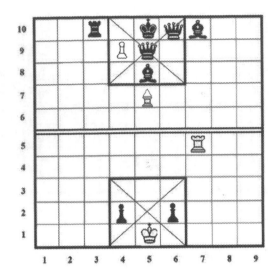

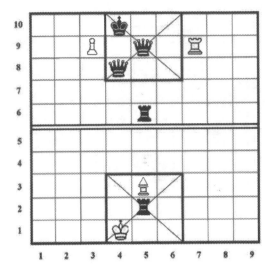

D 3.13.1

1	P4959+	Q6059
2	R7570#	
OR		
1	P4959	K5040,
2	R7545#"	

D 3.13.3

1	P3930+	K4049
2	R7959+	R5659
3	C5343#	
OR		
1	P3930	K4050,
2	R7970#	

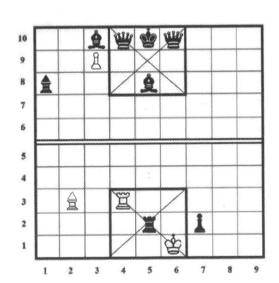

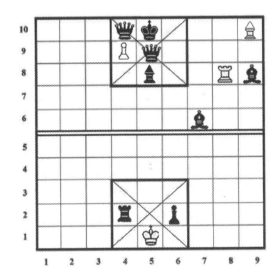

D 3.13.2

1	R4340+	K5040
2	C2320#	
OR		
1	R4340	K5059
2	C2320#"	

D 3.13.4

1	R8880+	B9870
2	R8070+	Q5960
3	P4959+	K5059
4	R7076#	
OR		
1	R8880+	Q5960,
2	P4959+	Q4059
3	3 R8089#	

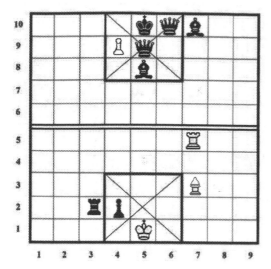

D 3.13.5

1	C7370+	B5870
2	P4959+	Q6059
3	R7570#	

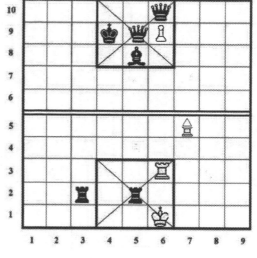

D 3.13.7

1	R6343+	Q5948
2	C7545+	Q4859
3	C4555+	Q5948
4	P6959+	Q6059
5	C5545#	

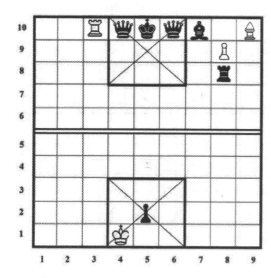

D 3.13.6

1	R3040+	K5059
2	C9099+	K5958
3	R4048#	

D 3.13.8

1	R8180+	Q5960
2	C7770+	Q6059
3	C7078+	Q5960
4	P4940+	K5059
5	R8089#	

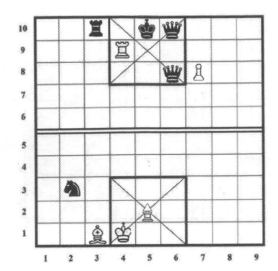

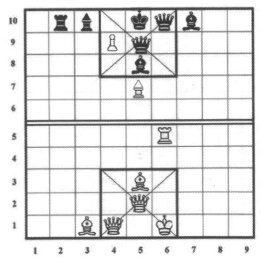

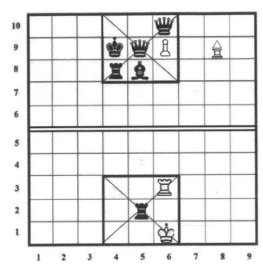

D 3.13.9

1	R4959+	K5059
2	B3153+	K5969
3	P7879#	

D 3.13.11

1	R6545	C3038
2	P4940+	R2040
3	R4565	R4047
4	R6560#	

D 3.13.10

1	P6959+	K4959
2	R6369+	K5950
3	C8980+	Q6059
4	R6960#	

D 3.13.12

1	P6960+	Q5960
2	R6360+	K5059
3	R6069#	

OR

1	R6960+	K5040
2	P6050#	

14. ROOK, KNIGHT AND CANNON

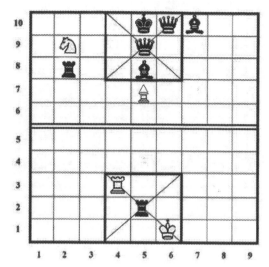

D 3.14.1

1 R4340#

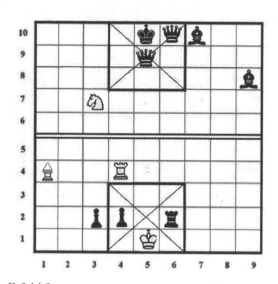

D 3.14.3

1	R4440+	k5040
2	N3729+	k4050
3	N2948+	k5040
4	C1444#	

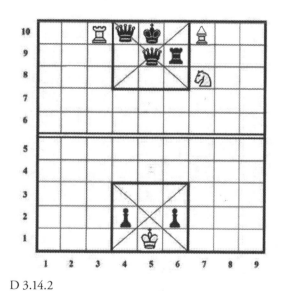

D 3.14.2

1	R3040+	K5040
2	N7760#	

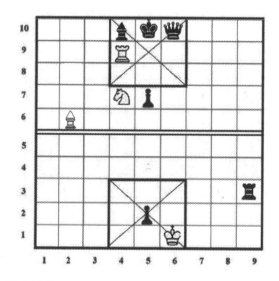

D 3.14.4

1	C2555+	P5756
2	N4768#	

OR

1	C2555+	Q6059
2	R4959#	

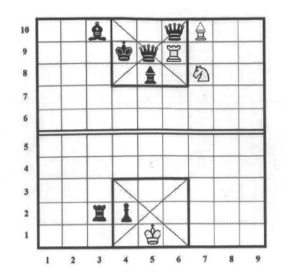

D 3.14.5

1	N7860+	K4948
2	C7078+	Q5968
3	R6949#	

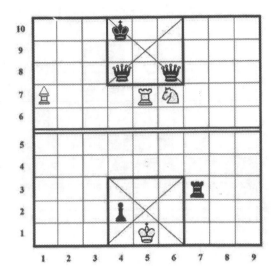

D 3.14.7

1	R5750+	K4049
2	R5040+	K4940
3	C1747+	Q4859
4	N6748#	

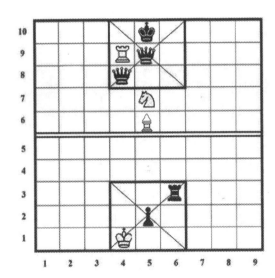

D 3.14.6

1	R4940+	K5040
2	N5738+	K4049
3	C5646#	

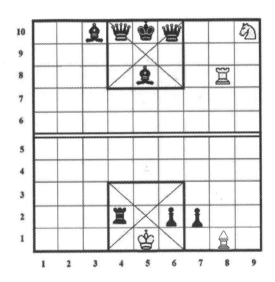

D 3.14.8

1	N9079+	K5059
2	R8858+	K5949
3	C8189+	Q4059
4	R5848+	K4948
5	N7967#	

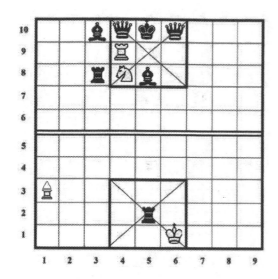

D 3.14.9

1	R4940+	K5059
2	R4050+	K5949
3	C1343+	K4948
4	R5040#	

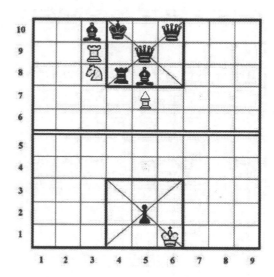

D 3.14.11

1	R3930+	K4049
2	R3040+	Q5940
3	N3820#	

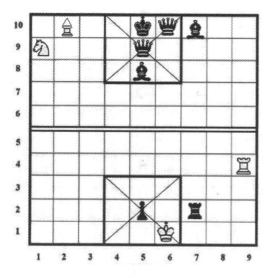

D 3.14.10

1	N1930+	Q5940
2	N3048+	K5059
3	R9399#	

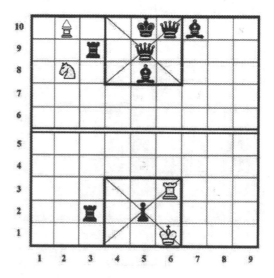

D 3.14.12

1	R6360+	Q5960
2	N2830#	

15.   ROOK, KNIGHT, CANNON AND PAWN

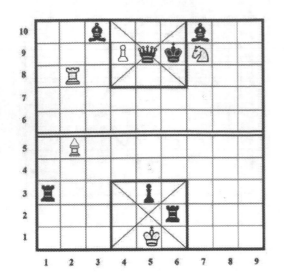

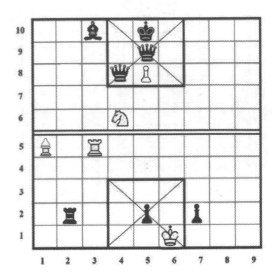

D 3.15.1

1	P4959+	K6960
2	R2868+	R6268
3	C2520+	B3018
4	N7950+	B1830
5	N5039+	B3018
6	P5950+	K6069
7	C2029#	

D 3.15.3

1	R3530+	Q5940
2	C1555+	Q4859
3	P5859+	K5059
4	R3039+	K5950
5	N4658+	Q4059
6	R3930#	

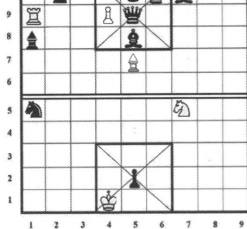

D 3.15.2

1	R1910	R2010
2	N7587	R1020
3	N8779#	

D 3.15.4

1	R7969+	K6050
2	P4959+	Q6859
3	R6959+	K5040
4	R5950+	K4049
5	N5637+	K4948
6	R5040#	

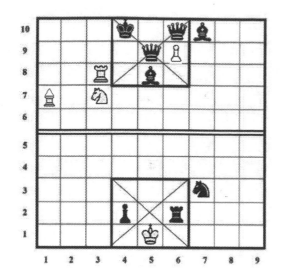

D 3.15.5

1	R3830+	B5830
2	N3729+	K4050
3	N2948+	K5040
4	C1747#	

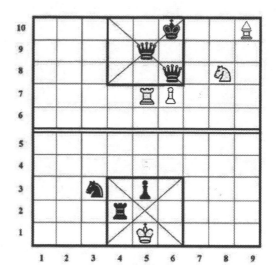

D 3.15.7

1	N8870+	K6069
2	P6768+	Q5968
3	N7088+	K6960
4	R5750	K6050
5	N8870#	

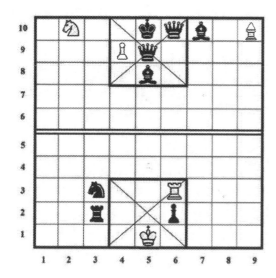

D 3.15.6

1	P4959+	K5059
2	N2038+	K5950
3	R6360#	

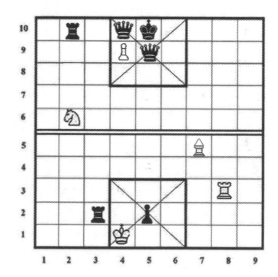

D 3.15.8

1	R8380+	Q5960
2	P4959+	K5059
3	N2647+	K5950
4	C7570+	Q6059
5	C7078+	Q5960
6	N4768+	K5059
7	R8089#	

CHAPTER 4   SOME BASIC END GAMES

1.   ONE PAWN

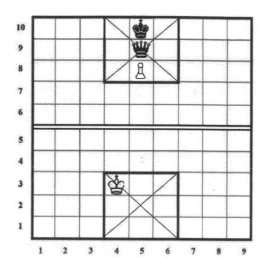

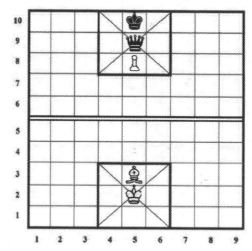

D 4.1.1   P vs. Q
1	K	4342	Q	5960
2	P	5868	Q	6059
3	P	6869	Q	5968
4	K	4241	Q	6859
5	K	4151	K	5040
6	P	6959 #		

D 4.1.3   P+B vs. Q
1	K	5251	Q	5940
2	P	5868	K	5060
3	K	5161	Q	4059
4	P	6869 +	K	6050
5	K	6151	Q	5948
6	K	5141	Q	4859
7	B	5371	Q	5948
8	K	4142	K	5040
9	P	6959 #		

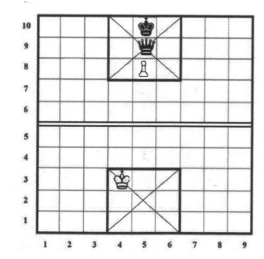

D 4.1.2   P vs. Q
1	K	4342	Q	5940
2	P	5868	K	5060
3	K	4252	Q	4059
4	P	6858	Q	5940
5	K	5242	K	6069
6	K	4252	K	6960 =

2. TWO PAWNS

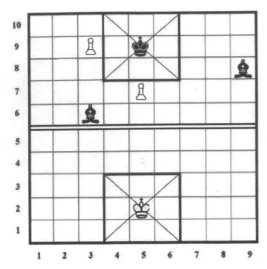

D 4.2.1   PP vs. BB

1	K	5242		B	3618
2	P	3949 +		K	5969
3	K	4252		B	1836
4	P	5767		B	3658
5	K	5262		B	9870
6	P	6768 +		K	6960
7	P	6869 +		K	6050
8	P	6960 #			

D 4.2.3   PP vs. P+Q

1	P	3949		K	6069
2	K	4252		P	4454
3	K	5251		Q	5960
4	K	5161		Q	6059
5	K	6151		Q	5960 =

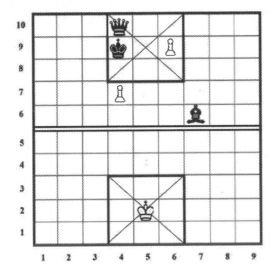

D 4.2.2   PP vs. BQ

1	K	5242		Q	4059
2	K	4241		B	7698
3	K	4151		Q	5940
4	K	5141		Q	4059 =

3. THREE PAWNS

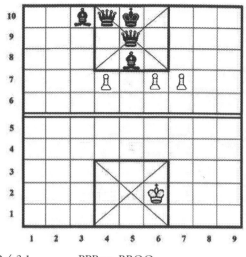

D 4.3.1   PPP vs. BBQQ

1	P	7778	B	5870
2	P	6768	B	7098
3	P	6869	B	9876
4	K	6252	B	3058
5	P	7879	Q	5968
6	P	4748	Q	4059
7	P	4849	Q	5948
8	P	7970	Q	6859
9	K	5262	B	7698
10	P	7060 +	Q	5960
11	P	6960 #		

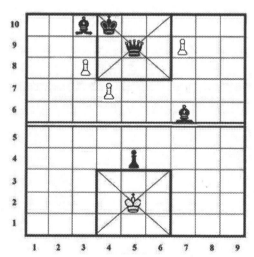

D 4.3.3   PPP vs. BBQQ

1	P	7778	B	9876
2	P	7879	B	7698
3	P	6960	Q	5960
4	P	7969	B	9876
5	P	6960	B	7698 =

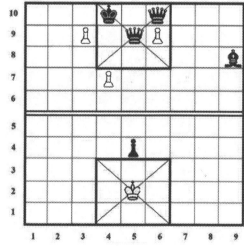

D 4.3.2   PPP vs. P+BQQ

1	K	5242	P	5747
2	K	4252	P	4757
3	P	6960	Q	5960
4	P	4748	Q	6059
5	P	4858	Q	5960
6	K	5242	P	5747
7	K	4241	B	9876 =

D 4.3.4   PPP vs. P+BBQ

1	P	7969	Q	5968
2	P	3839	B	3018
3	P	4757	K	4050
4	P	3949	P	5444
5	K	5242	B	1836
6	P	5767	Q	6859
7	P	6959 +	k	5060
8	P	6768 #		

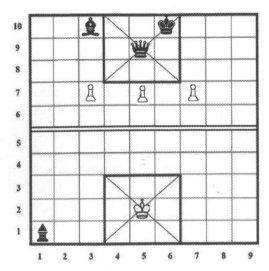

D 4.3.5		PPP vs. C+BQ			
1	P	3738		C	1117
2	P	7778		C	1718
3	P	3839		B	3058
4	P	5758		C	1878
5	P	5859		C	7879
6	P	3949		C	7970
7	P	4940		C	7040
8	P	5950 +		K	6069
9	P	5040 =			

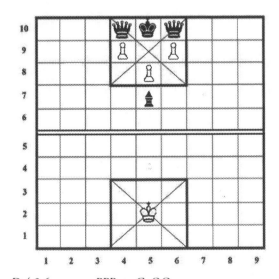

D 4.3.6		PPP vs. C+QQ			
1	K	5262		C	5767
2	K	6261		C	6766
3	K	6151		C	6665
4	P	4940+		K	5040
5	P	6960		K	4049=

4.   ONE KNIGHT

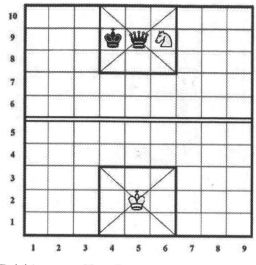

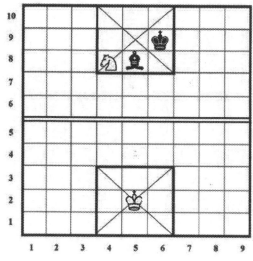

D 4.4.1   N vs. Q

1	N	6957 +		K	4948
2	N	5778		Q	5968
3	N	7866		Q	6859
4	N	6647		Q	5960
5	N	4728		Q	6059
6	N	2830 +		K	4849
7	N	3059		K	4940
8	N	5938 +		K	4049
9	N	3820 *			

D 4.4.3   N vs. B

1	N	4856		B	5830
2	N	5677 +		K	6960
3	N	7789 +		K	6069
4	K	5251		B	3018
5	N	8877 +		K	6960 =

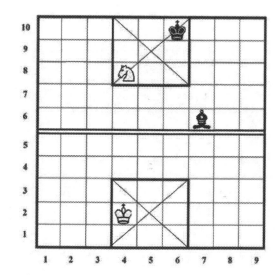

D 4.4.2

1	N	4867		K	6050
2	K	4241		K	5060
3	K	4151		B	7698
4	N	6788 *			

5. TWO KNIGHTS

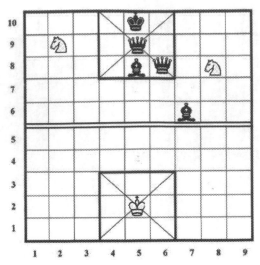

D 4.5.1		NN vs. BBQQ		
1	N	8890	B	5830
2	N	9079 +	K	5060
3	N	2937	Q	5940
4	N	3756	Q	6859
5	N	5677	B	3058
6	N	7789	K	6069
7	N	7967	Q	5968
8	N	6788 +	K	6959
9	N	8876 *		

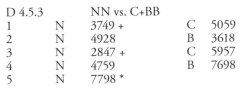

D 4.5.3		NN vs. C+BB		
1	N	3749 +	C	5059
2	N	4928	B	3618
3	N	2847 +	C	5957
4	N	4759	B	7698
5	N	7798 *		

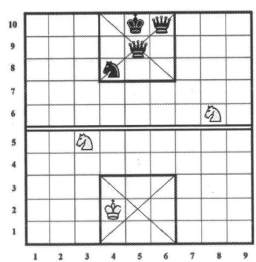

D 4.5.2		NN vs. N+QQ		
1	K	4252	K	5040
2	N	8678	K	4049
3	K	5242	K	4940
4	N	3527	K	4050
5	N	2739 +	k	5040
6	K	4241	K	4049
7	N	3927 *		

6.   ONE KNIGHT AND ONE PAWN

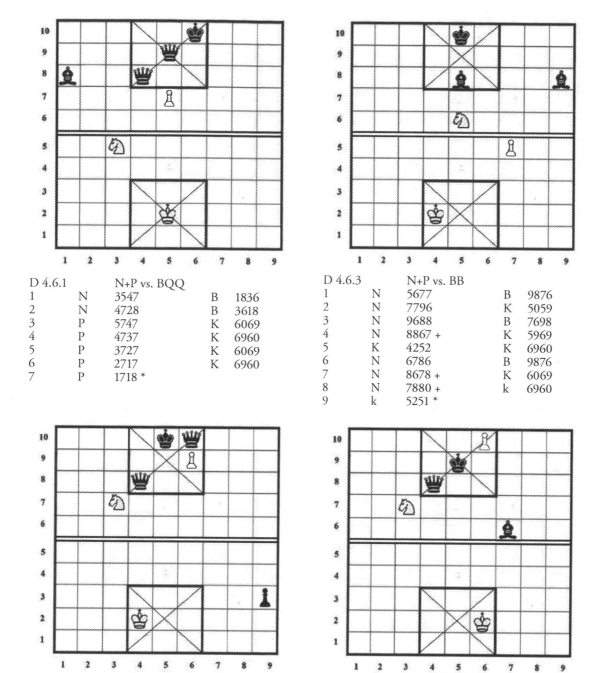

D 4.6.1		N+P vs. BQQ			
1	N	3547	B	1836
2	N	4728	B	3618
3	P	5747	K	6069
4	P	4737	K	6960
5	P	3727	K	6069
6	P	2717	K	6960
7	P	1718 *		

D 4.6.3		N+P vs. BB			
1	N	5677	B	9876
2	N	7796	K	5059
3	N	9688	B	7698
4	N	8867 +	K	5969
5	K	4252	K	6960
6	N	6786	B	9876
7	N	8678 +	K	6069
8	N	7880 +	k	6960
9	k	5251 *		

D 4.6.2		N+P vs. P+QQ			
1	N	3718	K	5040
2	N	1839	K	4049
3	N	3918	K	4940
4	N	1837	K	4050
5	K	4241	P	9392
6	N	3758	Q	6059
7	N	5846	Q	5960
8	N	4667	K	5040 =

D 4.6.4		N+P vs. BQ			
1	K	6261	B	7698
2	N	3756	K	5949
3	N	5668 +	K	4959
4	N	6887	K	5949
5	K	6151	Q	4859
6	P	6050	B	9870
7	N	8779	K	4948
8	N	7967 +	K	4849
9	N	6759 *		

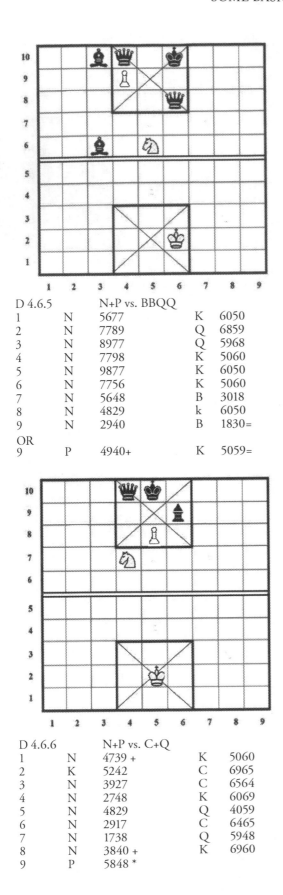

D 4.6.5   N+P vs. BBQQ

1	N	5677	K	6050
2	N	7789	Q	6859
3	N	8977	Q	5968
4	N	7798	K	5060
5	N	9877	K	6050
6	N	7756	K	5060
7	N	5648	B	3018
8	N	4829	k	6050
9	N	2940	B	1830=

OR

9	P	4940+	K	5059=

D 4.6.6   N+P vs. C+Q

1	N	4739 +	K	5060
2	K	5242	C	6965
3	N	3927	C	6564
4	N	2748	K	6069
5	N	4829	Q	4059
6	N	2917	C	6465
7	N	1738	Q	5948
8	N	3840 +	K	6960
9	P	5848 *		

7. ONE KNIGHT AND TWO PAWNS

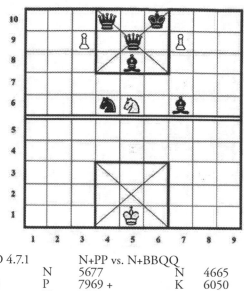

D 4.7.1		N+PP vs. N+BBQQ			
1	N	5677		N	4665
2	P	7969 +		K	6050
3	N	7789		N	6557
4	P	3949		N	5778
5	K	5152		B	7698
6	N	8977		B	9876
7	N	7796		N	7757
8	N	9688		B	5836
9	P	4939		N	5769
10	N	8869		B	3658=

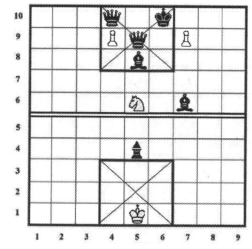

D 4.7.2		N+PP vs. C+BBQQ			
1	N	5677		C	5494
2	K	5141		K	6050
3	P	7969		C	9499
4	N	7756		Q	5948
5	N	5637		C	9949
6	N	3749		Q	4059
7	N	4928		Q	5960
8	N	2810		K	5040
9	N	1039		K	4049
10	N	3927		B	7698
11	N	2735		B	5876 =

8.   ONE CANNON

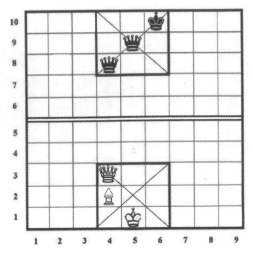

D 4.8.1   C+Q vs. QQ

1	Q	4352	K	6050
2	Q	5263	K	5060
3	C	4262 +	K	6050
4	C	6242	K	5060
5	C	4252	Q	5968
6	C	5262	Q	4859
7	C	6261	K	6050
8	C	6168 *		

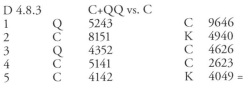

D 4.8.3   C+QQ vs. C

1	Q	5243	C	9646
2	C	8151	K	4940
3	Q	4352	C	4626
4	C	5141	C	2623
5	C	4142	K	4049 =

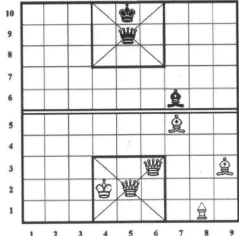

D 4.8.2   C+BBQQ vs. BQ

1	K	4243	K	5060
2	C	8161 +	K	6050
3	C	6141	K	5060
4	C	4161 +	K	6050
5	K	4353	K	5040
6	Q	5243	Q	5948
7	C	6141	K	4049
8	Q	4352 +	Q	4859
9	C	4151	B	7698
10	Q	5261	Q	5968 =

9. TWO CANNONS

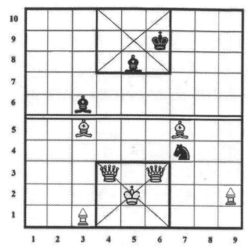

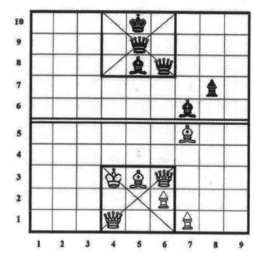

D 4.9.2   CC+BBQQ vs. N+BB
1	C	9291	N	7455
2	C	9151	N	5534
3	C	3121	N	3415
4	C	2124	N	1527
5	C	2454	B	5876
6	C	5434	B	3658
7	C	3474	N	2735
8	C	7476 *		

D 4.9.3   CC+BBQQ vs. C+BB
| 1 | C | 6252 | K | 5060, |
| 2 | C | 5292 | C | 8797= |

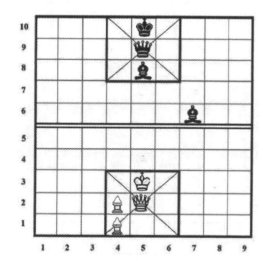

D 4.9.1   CC+Q vs. BBQQ
1	Q	5263	B	7698
2	C	4151	B	9876
3	K	5343	K	5060
4	C	4262	B	5870
5	C	6261	B	7098
6	K	4353	B	9870
7	C	5159 *		

10. ONE CANNON AND ONE PAWN

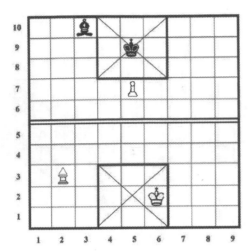

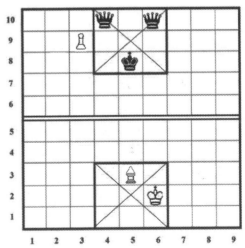

D 4.10.1   C+P vs. B

1	P	5747	B	3018
2	P	4748	B	1836
3	C	2327	K	5950
4	C	2747	K	5059
5	K	6261	K	5950
6	P	4849	B	3618
7	C	4727	B	1830
8	C	2729 #		

D 4.10.3   C+P+QQ vs. N+Q

1	C	6151	K	5060
2	P	5657	K	6050
3	P	5758	Q	5940
4	K	5242 +	K	5060
5	P	5848	N	3746
6	K	4252	Q	4059
7	C	5161 +	K	6050
8	P	4849	N	4638
9	P	4959 +	N	3859
10	C	6151 *		

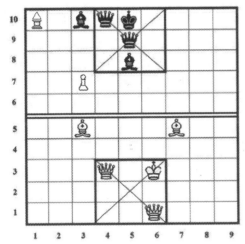

D 4.10.2   C+P+BBQQ vs. BBQQ

1	P	3738	B	5836
2	P	3839	Q	5948
3	P	3949	B	3658
4	C	1020	Q	4859
5	K	6353	Q	5968
6	P	4940 +	K	5059
7	P	4030	K	5969
8	K	5363	K	6959
9	C	2022	K	5950
10	C	2262	Q	6859
11	C	6252 #		

D 4.10.4   C+P vs. QQ

1	P	3949	K	5848
2	P	4939	Q	4059
3	C	5383	Q	5968
4	K	6252	Q	6859
5	C	8388	Q	5940
6	C	8880	Q	4059
7	K	5251	Q	5968 =

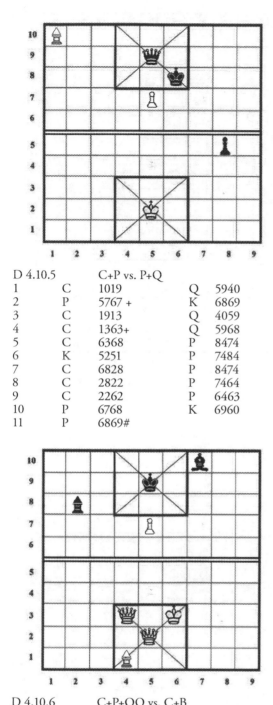

D 4.10.5   C+P vs. P+Q

1	C	1019	Q	5940
2	P	5767 +	K	6869
3	C	1913	Q	4059
4	C	1363+	Q	5968
5	C	6368	P	8474
6	K	5251	P	7484
7	C	6828	P	8474
8	C	2822	P	7464
9	C	2262	P	6463
10	P	6768	K	6960
11	P	6869#		

D 4.10.6   C+P+QQ vs. C+B

1	P	5747	K	5950
2	P	4748	C	2818
3	C	4151 +	K	5040
4	Q	5261	K	4050
5	P	4858 +	K	5040
6	P	5859	C	1848
7	Q	4352	C	4828
8	C	5141	C	2823
9	K	6362	C	2322 +
10	Q	5243 *		

11.   ONE CANNON AND TWO PAWNS

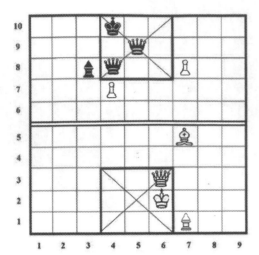

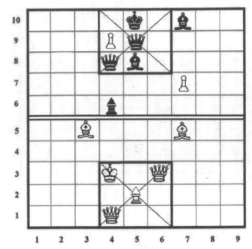

D 4.11.1		C+PP+BQ vs. C+QQ		
1	K	6252	C	3839
2	K	5253	C	3949
3	P	4737	C	4919
4	C	7141 +	K	4050
5	P	3738	K	5060
6	C	4161 +	K	6050
7	P	3848 *		

D 4.11.3		C+PP+BBQQ vs. C+BBQQ		
1	P	4939	C	4666
2	P	7778	C	6669
3	C	5232	C	6999
4	P	7879	Q	5968
5	P	7989	C	9996
6	K	4353	C	9616
7	C	3252	K	5040
8	P	3929	Q	4859 =

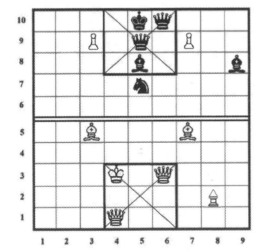

D 4.11.2		C+PP+BBQQ vs. N+BBQQ		
1	C	8252	B	9876
2	P	3949	Q	5948
3	P	7969	Q	6059
4	B	3553	N	5778
5	C	5212	N	7857
6	C	1210	Q	5968
7	P	4939	Q	6859 =

12. ONE ROOK

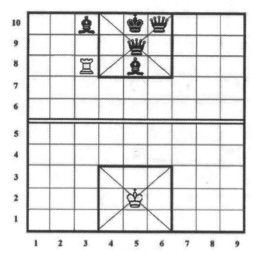

D 4.12.1   R vs. BBQQ

1	K	5251	K	5040
2	K	5152	K	4050
3	K	5242	Q	5940
4	K	4252	Q	4059
5	K	5242	Q	5940
6	R	3848	Q	4059
7	R	4849	B	5876
8	R	4939	B	7658 =

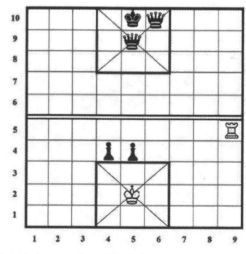

D 4.12.3   R vs. N+C

1	R	5954	K	4849
2	R	5424	N	2647
3	R	2429 +	K	4948
4	R	2920	C	4049
5	R	2030	C	4959
6	R	3040 +	C	5949
7	K	5242 *		

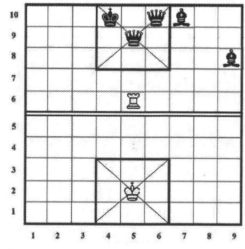

D 4.12.2   R vs. BBQQ

1	K	5251	K	4049
2	R	5646 +	Q	5948
3	K	5141	Q	6059
4	R	4616	Q	5968
5	R	1618	Q	6859
6	R	1819 +	K	4940
7	R	1959 *		

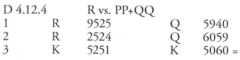

D 4.12.4   R vs. PP+QQ

1	R	9525	Q	5940
2	R	2524	Q	6059
3	K	5251	K	5060 =

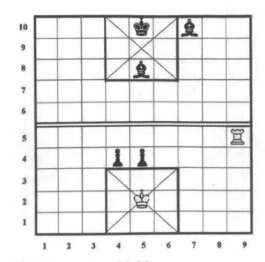

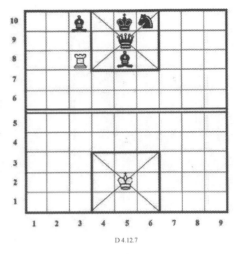

D 4.12.7

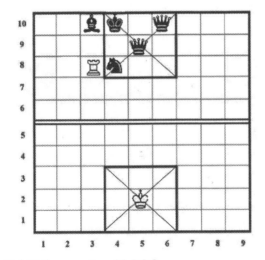

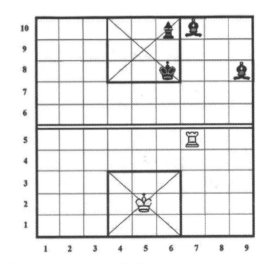

D 4.12.5		R vs. PP+BB		
1	R	9525	K	5059
2	R	2529 +	K	5950
3	R	2924	K	5059 =

D 4.12.7		R vs. N+BBQ		
1	K	5251	N	6089
2	R	3837	N	8960
3	R	3787	N	6078
4	R	8788	N	7860
5	R	8880	K	5040 =

D 4.12.6		R vs. N+BQQ		
1	K	5251	B	3058
2	K	5141	K	4050
3	R	3828	B	5830
4	K	4151	K	5040
5	R	2838	B	3058 =

D 4.12.8		R vs. C+BB		
1	R	7578 +	K	6869
2	R	7879 +	K	6968
3	K	5251	C	6050
4	R	7977	C	5060
5	K	5152	K	6869
6	R	7778	C	6050
7	R	7877	C	5060
8	R	7778	C	6050 =

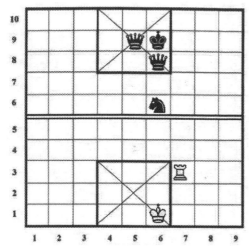

D 4.12.9		R vs. N+QQ		
1	R	7376	N	6647
2	R	7656	N	4735
3	R	5636	N	3554
4	R	3676	N	5442 +
5	K	6162	N	4254 +
6	K	6261	Q	5948
7	R	7679 +	K	6960
8	R	7978	Q	4859
9	R	7870 +	K	6069
10	R	7079 +	K	6960
11	R	7959 *		

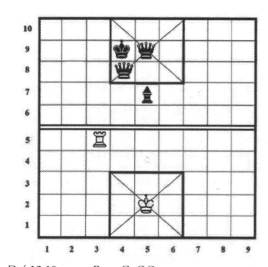

D 4.12.10		R vs. C+QQ		
1	K	5242	C	5747
2	R	3537	C	4746
3	R	3747	C	4656
4	R	4746	C	5657
5	R	4616	C	5747
6	K	4241	C	4745 =

13. TWO ROOKS

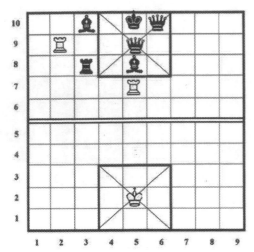

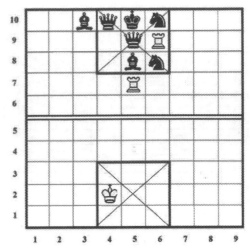

D 4.13.1   RR vs. R+BBQQ

1	R	2949	R	3848	
2	R	4939	K	5040	
3	R	5787	K	4050	
4	R	8789	K	5040	
5	K	5251	R	4841	+
6	K	5152	R	4148	=

D 4.13.3   RR vs. NN+BBQQ

1	R	5747	N	6089	
2	R	6979	B	3018	
3	R	4746	N	8997	
4	R	4696	N	9776	
5	R	9690 +	Q	5960	
6	R	7949	Q	4059	
7	R	9094	B	5836	
8	R	4946	B	3658	
9	R	9454	B	1836	
10	R	4647 *			

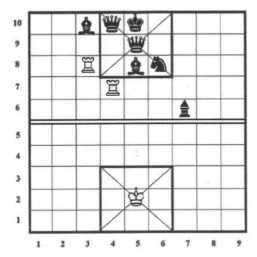

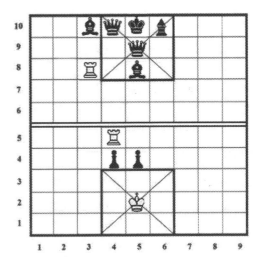

D 4.13.2   RR vs. N+C+BBQQ

1	R	4749	C	7679	
2	R	4947	C	7976	
3	R	3836	K	5060	
4	R	3666	K	6050	
5	R	4767	C	7670	
6	R	6686	C	7060 =	

D 4.13.4   RR vs. C+PP+BBQQ

1	R	4549	C	6069	
2	R	4947	C	6968	
3	R	3837	C	6860	
4	R	4767	C	6070 =	

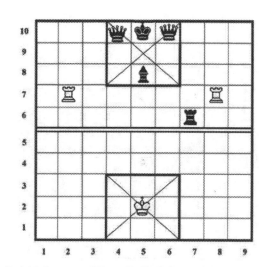

D 4.13.5		RR vs. R+N+QQ		
1	R	7078	N	3840
2	R	7848	R	6967
3	K	5141	N	4029
4	R	4849	R	6727
5	R	4939	R	2747 +
6	K	4151	R	4727
7	R	5646	R	2757 +
8	K	5141	R	5727
9	R	4649 *		

D 4.13.6		RR vs. R+C+QQ		
1	R	8788	R	7656+
2	K	5262	C	5848
3	R	2767	Q	4059
4	R	8887	C	4840
5	R	6727	Q	5948
6	R	8767	Q	4859
7	R	6757	R	5657
8	R	2757	C	4048
9	K	6252	K	5040 =

14. ONE ROOK AND ONE PAWN

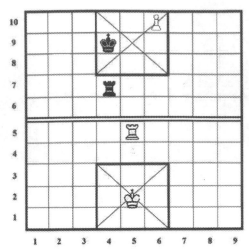

D 4.14.1   R+P vs. R

1	P	6050		R	4746
2	R	5559 +		K	4948
3	P	5040		R	4647
4	P	4030		R	4746
5	R	5950		K	4849
6	R	5040 #			

D 4.14.3   R+P vs. BBQQ

1	R	5747		B	7098
2	K	5242		B	9870
3	P	4940 +		Q	5940
4	R	4740 +		K	5059
5	K	4252 *			

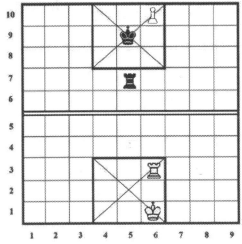

D 4.14.2   R+P vs. R

1	R	6369 +		K	5958
2	P	6050		R	5756
3	P	5040		R	5657
4	R	6960		K	5848
5	P	4030		K	4849
6	R	5040 +		K	4959
7	R	4060		R	5756
8	P	3040		K	5949 =

D 4.14.4   R+P vs. N+BBQQ

1	P	3738		B	5836
2	P	3839		B	3058
3	P	3949		Q	5940
4	R	5424		Q	6059
5	R	2420		N	7655
6	P	4959 +		K	5059
7	R	2040 *			

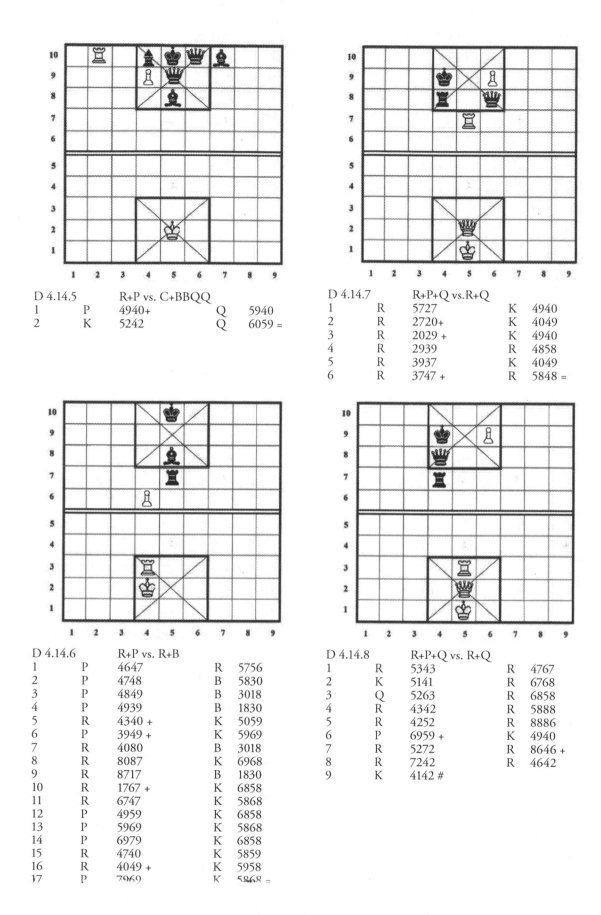

D 4.14.5   R+P vs. C+BBQQ
1   P   4940+   Q   5940
2   K   5242   Q   6059 =

D 4.14.7   R+P+Q vs.R+Q
1   R   5727   K   4940
2   R   2720+   K   4049
3   R   2029 +   K   4940
4   R   2939   R   4858
5   R   3937   K   4049
6   R   3747 +   R   5848 =

D 4.14.6   R+P vs. R+B
1   P   4647   R   5756
2   P   4748   B   5830
3   P   4849   B   3018
4   P   4939   B   1830
5   R   4340 +   K   5059
6   P   3949 +   K   5969
7   R   4080   B   3018
8   R   8087   K   6968
9   R   8717   B   1830
10   R   1767 +   K   6858
11   R   6747   K   5868
12   P   4959   K   6858
13   P   5969   K   5868
14   P   6979   K   6858
15   R   4740   K   5859
16   R   4049 +   K   5958
17   P   7969   K   5868 =

D 4.14.8   R+P+Q vs. R+Q
1   R   5343   R   4767
2   K   5141   R   6768
3   Q   5263   R   6858
4   R   4342   R   5888
5   R   4252   R   8886
6   P   6959 +   K   4940
7   R   5272   R   8646 +
8   R   7242   R   4642
9   K   4142 #

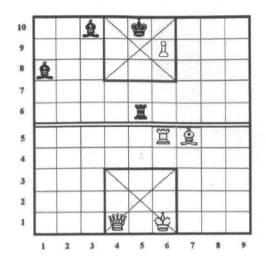

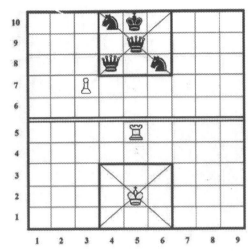

D 4.14.9		R+P+BQ vs. R+BB		
1	B	7553	R	5657
2	Q	4152	R	5756
3	K	6151	R	5657
4	R	6575	K	5040
5	R	7545 +	K	4050
6	K	5141	R	5756
7	R	4540 #		

D 4.14.11		R+P vs. NN+QQ		
1	R	5595	K	5060
2	R	9590 +	K	6069
3	K	5262	N	4029
4	P	3747	N	2817
5	P	4748	Q	5948
6	R	9098	Q	4859
7	R	9899 +	K	6960
8	R	9959	N	1736
9	R	5958 *		

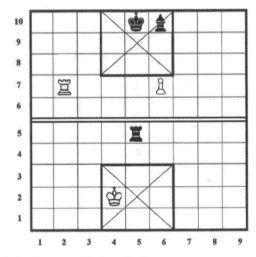

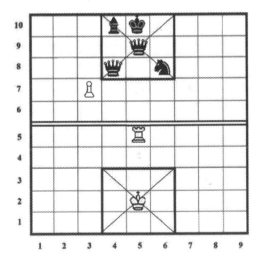

D 4.14.10		R+P vs. R+C		
1	R	2747	R	5556
2	P	6768	R	5655
3	R	4748	R	5556
4	P	6869	R	5655 =

D 4.14.12		R+P vs. N+C+QQ		
1	P	3738	K	5060
2	R	5565	K	6069
3	K	5262	C	4060
4	R	6575	C	6010
5	R	7578	C	1018
6	R	7879 +	K	6960
7	R	7970	K	6069
8	R	7010 *		

15. ONE ROOK AND TWO PAWNS

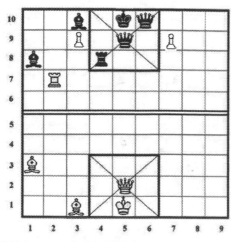

D 4.15.1		R+PP+BBQQ vs. R+BBQQ			
1	R	2787	R	4878
2	P	7969	R	7868
3	R	8789	Q	5948
4	P	3949	B	1836
5	P	6979	R	6878
6	B	3153	B	3618
7	P	7969	R	7868
8	B	5375	B	1836
9	R	8986	R	6869
10	R	8656 +	B	3658
11	R	5658 +	Q	6059 =

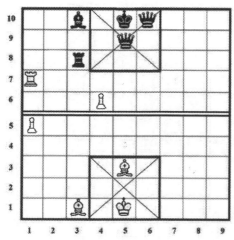

D 4.15.2		R+PP+BB vs. R+BQQ			
1	R	1727	R	3818
2	R	2725	B	3058
3	R	2520	Q	5940
4	R	2025	R	1817
5	R	2555	Q	4059
6	B	5331	K	5040
7	R	5565	K	4050
8	P	4647	B	5830
9	P	4748	R	1757 +
10	K	5141	Q	5948 =

16.   ONE KNIGHT AND ONE CANNON

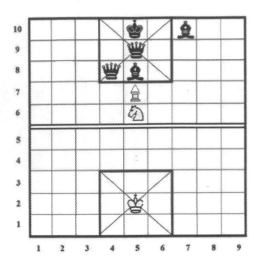

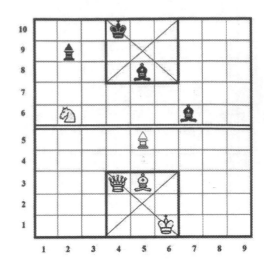

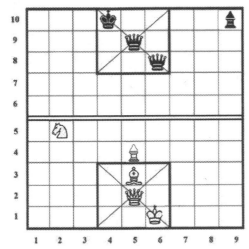

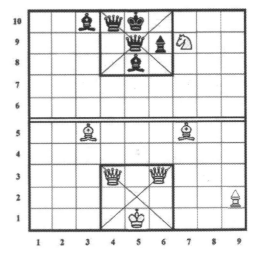

D 4.16.1		N+C vs. BBQQ		
1	K	5262	K	5040
2	N	5637	Q	5960
3	N	3729 +	K	4049
4	C	5747 +	K	4959
5	N	2948 *		

D 4.16.3		N+C+BQ vs. C+QQ		
1	N	2517	C	9099
2	N	1738 +	K	4049
3	C	5444	C	9998
4	N	3746 +	Q	5948
5	C	4442	K	4959
6	N	4627	K	5950
7	Q	5243	Q	4859
8	N	2738 +	K	5060
9	C	4262 #		

D 4.16.2		N+C+BQ vs. C+BB		
1	N	2638 +	C	2939
2	C	5557	K	4049
3	B	5375	B	5836
4	C	5767	K	4948
5	C	6762	K	4858
6	C	6272	B	7698
7	C	7222	C	3949
8	C	2228 +	C	4948
9	N	3840 +	K	5859
10	C	2898 *		

D 4.16.4		N+C+BBQQ vs. C+BBQQ		
1	C	9262	K	5060
2	C	6222	C	6968
3	C	2220	C	6869
4	N	7987	C	6989
5	N	8766	B	5876
6	N	6647	C	8969
7	N	4728	B	7658 =

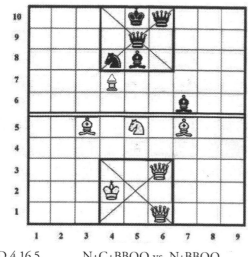

D 4.16.5   N+C+BBQQ vs, N+BBQQ
1   N   5567   B   5870
2   N   6779 +   N   4869
3   C   4787   Q   5968
4   C   8757   B   7698
5   C   5751   B   9876
6   N   7987   B   7098
7   N   8768 *

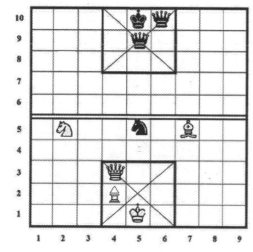

D 4.16.6   N+C+BQ vs. N+QQ
1   N   2537   N   5563 +
2   C   4262   K   5040
3   N   3729 +   K   4049
4   Q   4352   N   6355
5   C   6264   N   5534
6   C   6467   N   3446
7   C   6717   N   4637
8   C   1712   Q   5948
9   Q   5243   Q   6059
10   C   1242   N   3726
11   Q   4352 +   N   2647
12   C   4212 *

17. ONE KNIGHT, ONE CANNON AND ONE PAWN

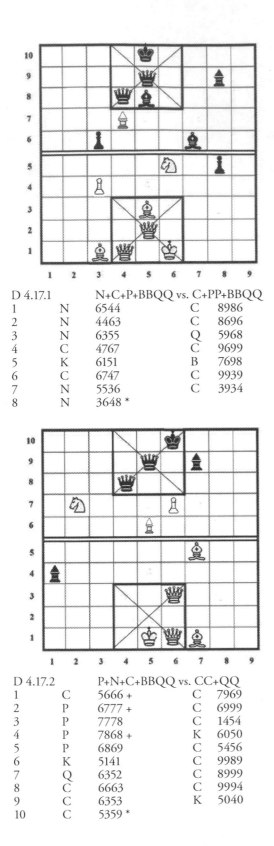

D 4.17.1		N+C+P+BBQQ vs.	C+PP+BBQQ	
1	N	6544	C	8986
2	N	4463	C	8696
3	N	6355	Q	5968
4	C	4767	C	9699
5	K	6151	B	7698
6	C	6747	C	9939
7	N	5536	C	3934
8	N	3648 *		

D 4.17.2		P+N+C+BBQQ vs.	CC+QQ	
1	C	5666 +	C	7969
2	P	6777 +	C	6999
3	P	7778	C	1454
4	P	7868 +	K	6050
5	P	6869	C	5456
6	K	5141	C	9989
7	Q	6352	C	8999
8	C	6663	C	9994
9	C	6353	K	5040
10	C	5359 *		

18. ONE KNIGHT, ONE CANNON AND TWO PAWNS

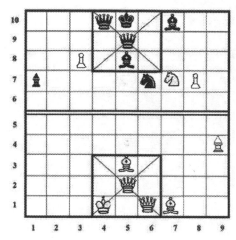

D 4.18.1		N+C+PP+BBQQ	vs.	N+C+BBQQ
1	N	7789	C	1719
2	C	9490 +	Q	5960
3	N	8968 +	C	1969
4	P	8777	N	6755
5	N	6887	N	5547
6	N	8779	N	4766
7	P	7767	N	6647
8	C	9099	K	5059
9	C	9997	N	4755
10	P	6768 *		

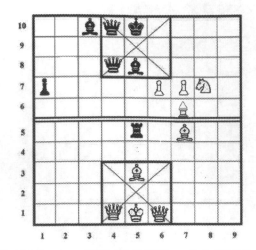

D 4.18.2		N+C+PP+BBQQ vs.	R+P+BBQQ	
1	C	7696	R	5556
2	N	8779 +	K	5060
3	C	9693	P	1716
4	C	9363	R	5666
5	Q	6152	P	1615
6	P	6757	R	6656
7	P	5758	Q	4059
8	P	5848	R	5676
9	P	7767 +	R	7666
10	P	4849	K	6069
11	N	7998	Q	5948
12	P	6768 +	K	6960
13	P	6869 +	K	6050
14	P	6960 #		

19.   ONE ROOK AND ONE KNIGHT

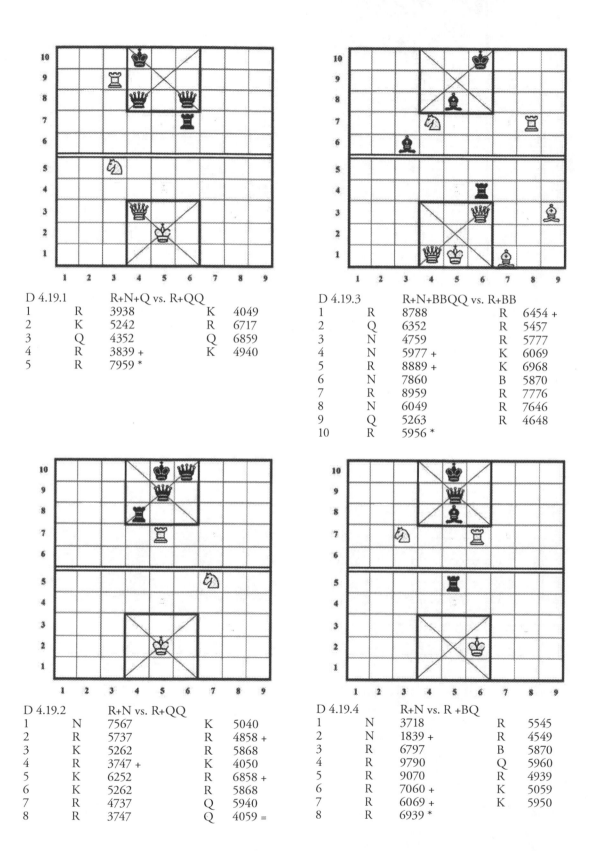

D 4.19.1		R+N+Q vs. R+QQ		
1	R	3938	K	4049
2	K	5242	R	6717
3	Q	4352	Q	6859
4	R	3839 +	K	4940
5	R	7959 *		

D 4.19.3		R+N+BBQQ vs. R+BB		
1	R	8788	R	6454 +
2	Q	6352	R	5457
3	N	4759	R	5777
4	N	5977 +	K	6069
5	R	8889 +	K	6968
6	N	7860	B	5870
7	R	8959	R	7776
8	N	6049	R	7646
9	Q	5263	R	4648
10	R	5956 *		

D 4.19.2		R+N vs. R+QQ		
1	N	7567	K	5040
2	R	5737	R	4858 +
3	K	5262	R	5868
4	R	3747 +	K	4050
5	K	6252	R	6858 +
6	K	5262	R	5868
7	R	4737	Q	5940
8	R	3747	Q	4059 =

D 4.19.4		R+N vs. R +BQ		
1	N	3718	R	5545
2	N	1839 +	R	4549
3	R	6797	B	5870
4	R	9790	Q	5960
5	R	9070	R	4939
6	R	7060 +	K	5059
7	R	6069 +	K	5950
8	R	6939 *		

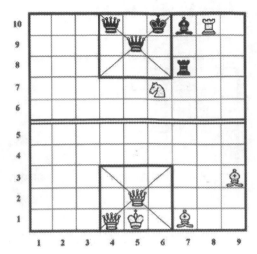

D 4.19.5   R+N+BBQQ vs. R+BQQ

1	N	6788	K	6069
2	N	8870	R	7879
3	R	8090	Q	5968
4	Q	5243	Q	4059
5	B	9375	Q	5940
6	N	7099	R	7989
7	R	9040	Q	6859
8	R	4050	K	6968
9	R	5090	K	6869
10	B	7593	K	6968 =

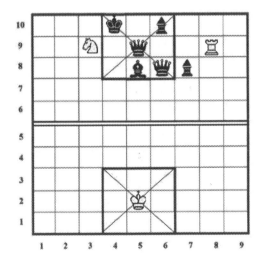

D 4.19.6   R+N vs. CC+BQQ

1	R	8987	K	4049
2	R	8747 +	Q	5948
3	K	5242	Q	6859
4	R	4727	C	7870
5	N	3918	K	4940
6	N	1837	B	5830
7	N	3729 +	K	4050
8	R	2757 *		

20. ONE ROOK, ONE KNIGHT AND ONE PAWN

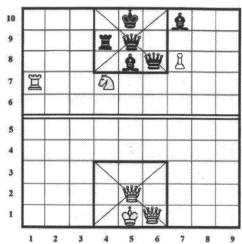

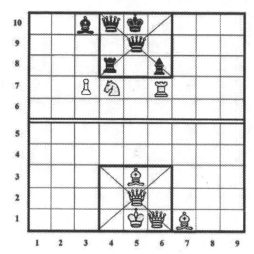

D 4.20.1		R+N+P+QQ vs. R+BBQQ		
1	N	4768 +	Q	5968
2	P	7868	R	4939
3	P	6869	B	5830
4	R	1757 +	K	5040
5	P	6959	R	3931 +
6	Q	5241	R	3141 +
7	K	5152	R	4146
8	P	5969	K	4049
9	R	5759 +	K	4948
10	R	5950 *		

D 4.20.3		R+N+P+BBQQ vs. R+C+BQQ		
1	R	6765	C	6860
2	R	6515	C	6069
3	R	1510	B	3018
4	N	4735	C	6979
5	N	3527	R	4828 =

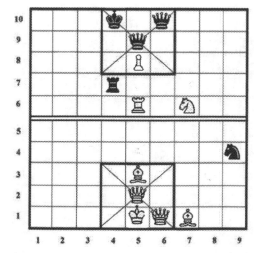

D 4.20.2		R+N+P+BBQQ vs. R+N+QQ		
1	P	5859	Q	6059
2	R	5659	R	4748
3	B	5331	N	9486
4	Q	5243	N	8678
5	R	5956	K	4049
6	B	3113	K	4940
7	N	7668 *		

21. ONE ROOK AND ONE CANNON

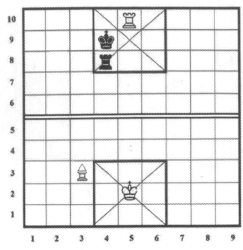

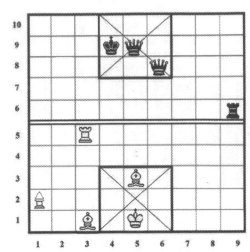

D 4.21.1   R+C vs. R

1	C	3330		R	4842 +
2	K	5251		R	4247
3	C	3040		R	4737
4	R	5056 *			

D 4.21.3   R+C+BB vs. R+QQ

1	R	3545 +		Q	5948
2	C	1343		R	9691 +
3	B	5371		R	9171 +
4	K	5152		R	7172 +
5	K	5253		R	7274
6	R	4575 +		R	7444
7	R	7578		Q	6859
8	R	7858 *			

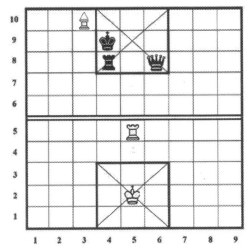

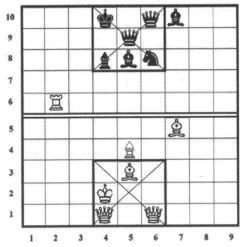

D 4.21.2   R+C vs. R+Q

1	R	5550		R	4828
2	C	3040		Q	6859
3	C	4030		Q	5968
4	R	5054		R	2848
5	C	3080		R	4842 +
6	K	5251		R	4248
7	C	8088		R	4846
8	R	5458		R	4647
9	R	5868		R	4757 +
10	K	5161		K	4959 =

D 4.21.4   R+C+BBQQ vs. N+C+BBQQ

1	R	2620 +		K	4049
2	K	4252		N	6856
3	C	5455		N	5637
4	R	2027		N	3745
5	R	2747		N	4533 +
6	R	4743		N	3325
7	B	5335		N	2517
8	R	4347		N	1736
9	C	5545		Q	5968
10	R	4746 *			

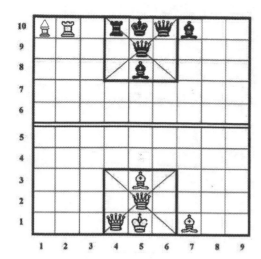

D 4.21.5   R+C+BBQQ vs. R+BBQQ
1   K   5161   B   7098
2   K   6162   B   9870
3   C   1040   Q   5940
4   R   2028   Q   6059 =

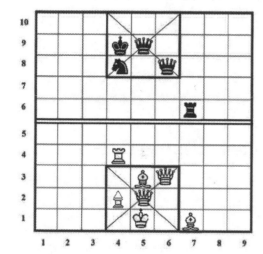

D 4.21.6   R+C+BBQQ vs. R+N+QQ
1   B   5375   R   7656
2   K   5141   R   5655
3   B   7193   R   5556
4   R   4454 +   R   5646
5   R   5414   R   4645
6   R   1413   R   4546
7   Q   5243   R   4666
8   K   4151   R   6636
9   Q   4352 +   R   3646 =

22. ONE ROOK, ONE CANNON AND ONE PAWN

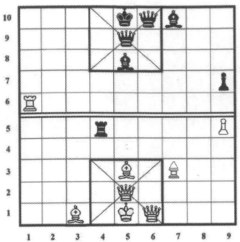

D 4.22.1		R+C+P+BBQQ	vs.	R+P+BBQQ	
1	B	5375		R	4547
2	C	7353		K	5040
3	R	1610 +		K	4049
4	C	5343 +		R	4777
5	B	3153		R	7757
6	C	4341		R	5767
7	Q	5243 +		Q	5948
8	R	1018		Q	6059
9	Q	4352 +		R	6747
10	R	1819 +		K	4940
11	R	1959		R	4745
12	R	5999		K	4050
13	R	9997 *			

D 4.22.3		R+C+P+BBQQ	vs.	R+C+QQ	
1	K	5152		R	6463
2	C	7177		R	6367
3	C	7778		C	8188
4	C	7838		C	8858 +
5	B	5335		R	6757 +
6	K	5242		R	5737
7	R	9290 +		K	6069
8	R	9099 +		K	6960
9	C	3830 +		R	3730
10	P	4959		Q	4059
11	R	9990 +		K	6069
12	R	9030 *			

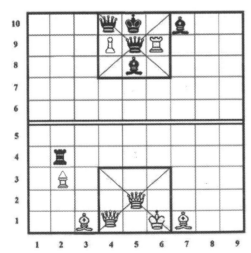

D 4.22.2		R+C+P+BBQQ	vs.	R+BBQQ	
1	C	2333		R	2434
2	C	3323		R	3424
3	C	2333		R	2434
4	C	3323		R	3424
5	C	2333		R	2434
6	C	3323 **			

CHAPTER 5   THE OPENING

1.   THE FLOW CHART OF THE OPENING SYSTEMS

A. White's First Opening Move (6 Regular Openings):
   1. Center Cannon Opening
   2. Palace Corner Cannon Opening
   3. Cross Palace Cannon Opening
   4. Pawn Opening
   5. Bishop Opening
   6. Knight Opening

B. Black's First Opening Response (vs. Center Cannon Opening):
   1. Knight's Response
   2. Cannons Game
   3. Cannon Counter Attack

C. The Knight's Response (vs. Center Cannon Opening):
   1. Double-Knights Defense
   2. Elbow Knight Defense
   3. Palace Knight Defense
   4. Single Knight Defense

D. Some Popular Double-Knights Defense Systems (vs. Center Cannon Opening)

E. Some Popular Offense Systems (vs. Double-Knights Defense)

2. THE REGULAR OPENINGS

D 5.2.1 CENTER CANNON OPENING

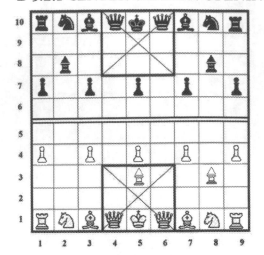

D 5.2.2 PALACE CORNER OPENING

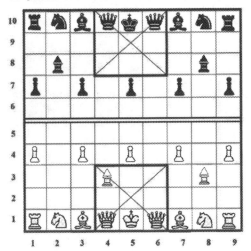

D 5.2.3 CROSS PALACE CANNON OPENING

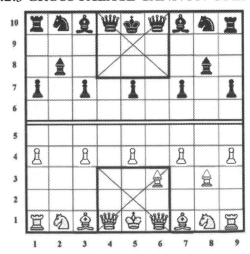

D 5.2.4 PAWN OPENING

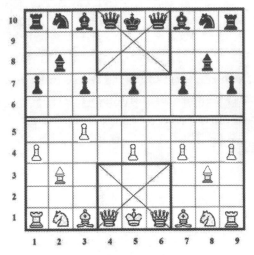

D 5.2.5 BISHOP OPENING

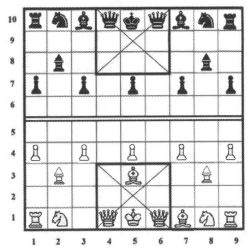

D 5.2.6 KNIGHT OPENING

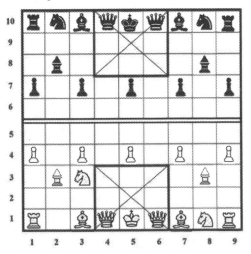

3. SOME IRREGULAR OPENINGS

D 5.3.1 KING'S PAWN OPENING

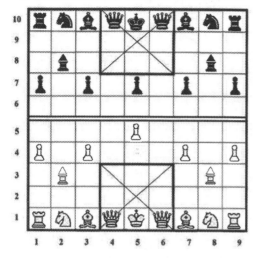

D 5.3.2 EDGED PAWN OPENING

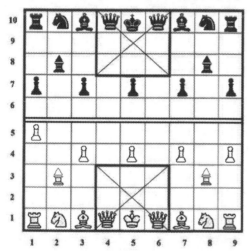

D 5.3.3 EDGED KNIGHT OPENING

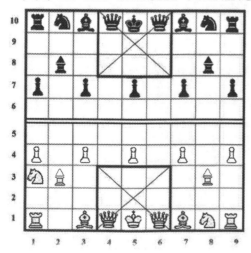

D 5.3.4 EDGED BISHOP OPENING

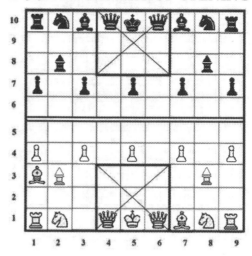

D 5.3.5 IRREGULAR CANNON OPENINGS

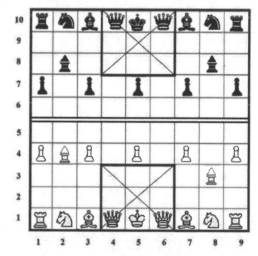

D 5.3.6 KING OPENING

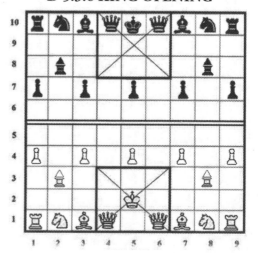

4. CENTER CANNON OPENING

D 5.4.1 1 C2353/C8353

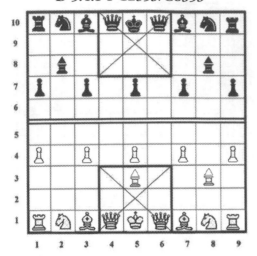

This Center Cannon Opening has been playing by most of Chinese Chess players in the past and present. White starts the game by placing one of the Cannons to the center @53. The following three are the most popular Black's opening responses against Center Cannon Opening.

D 5.4.3 CANNONS GAME

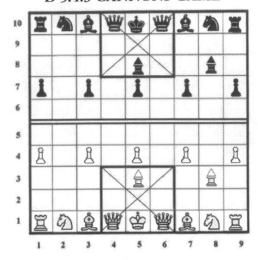

Black responses White's opening with a Cannon to the center @58, as well from the same direction as the White Cannon.

D 5.4.2 KNIGHT'S RESPONSE

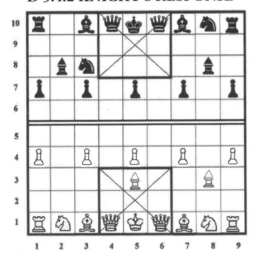

Black puts one or two Knights to guard the King's Pawn @57. This is the most used defensive systems against White's powerful and aggressive Center Cannon Opening.

D 5.4.4 CANNON COUNTER ATTACK

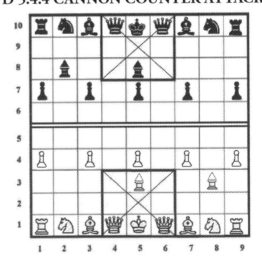

Black responses White's Center Cannon Opening with a Cannon to the center @58 from the opposite direction.

5. PALACE CORNER CANNON OPENING

D 5.5.1 1 C2343/C8363

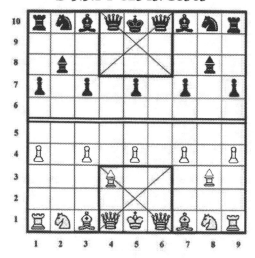

Palace Corner Cannon Opening is one of White's openings that places one Cannon at the near corner square of the palace (@43 or @63). The following three are the popular defensive systems vs. this Opening.

D 5.5.3 CANNON CENTER DEFENSE

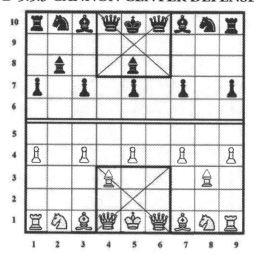

| 1 C2343 | C2858/8858 |
| Or 1 C8363 | C8858/2858 |

D 5.5.2 ROOK DEFENSE

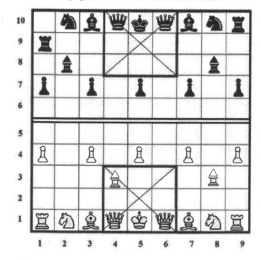

| 1 C2343 | R1019 |
| Or 1 C8363 | R9099 |

D 5.5.4 PAWN DEFENSE

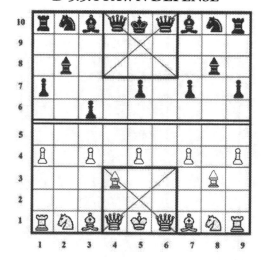

| 1 C2343 | P3736/7776 |
| Or 1C8363 | P7776/3736 |

6. CROSS PALACE CANNON OPENING

D 5.6.1 1 C2363/C8343

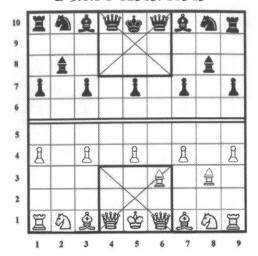

D 5.6.3 CANNON CENTER DEFENSE

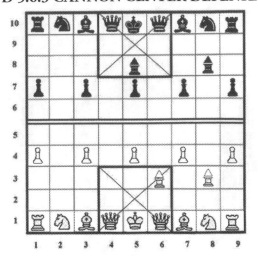

Cross Palace Cannon Opening is one of the Cannon openings. Starting a Cannon across the Palace area and placing it at the far Palace corner square (@43 or @63), is popular as of late. The following three are the popular defensive systems vs. this Opening.

1 C2363	C2858/8858
Or C8343	C8858/2858

D 5.6.2 ROOK DEFENSE

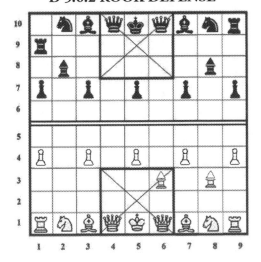

D 5.6.4 PAWN DEFENSE

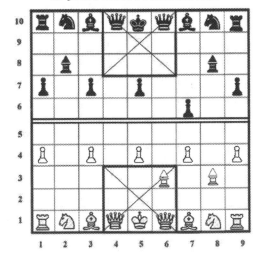

1 C2363	R1019
Or 1 C8343	R9099

1 C2363	P7776/3736
Or C8343	P3736/7776

7. PAWN OPENING

D 5.7.1 1 P3435/P7475

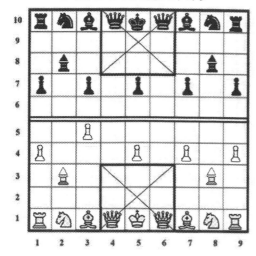

D 5.7.3 CANNON CENTER DEFENSE

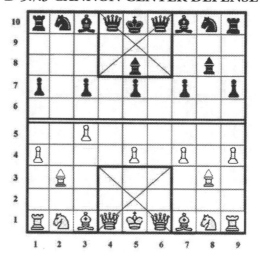

Pawn Opening is one of the popular openings for White to test Black's defense plans. The Pawn has to be one of the Bishop Pawns. The following three are the popular defensive systems vs. this Opening.

| 1 P3435 | C2858/8858 |
| Or 1 P7475 | C8858/2858 |

D 5.7.2 CANNON DEFENSE

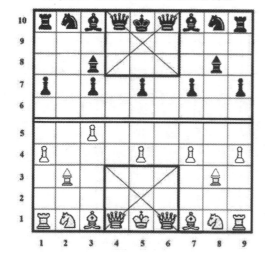

D 5.7.4 PAWNS GAME

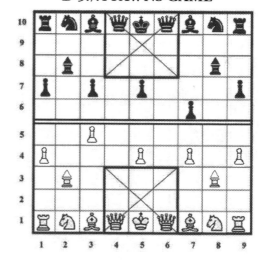

| 1P3435 | C2838 |
| Or 1 P7475 | C8878 |

| 1 P 3435 | P7776 |
| Or 1 P7475 | P3736 |

8. BISHOP OPENING

D 5.8.1 1 B3153/B7153

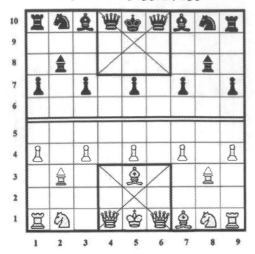

Bishop Opening is one of the widely used Openings. White starts the game by placing one of the two Bishops to @53. The following three are the popular Black's replies to Bishop Opening.

D 5.8.3 CANNON CENTER DEFENSE

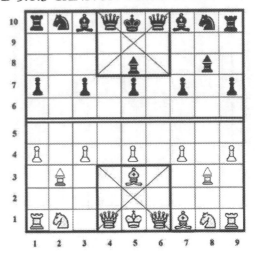

| 1 B3153 | C2858/8858 |
| Or 1 B7153 | C8858/2858 |

D 5.8.2 CROSS PALACE CANNON DEFENSE

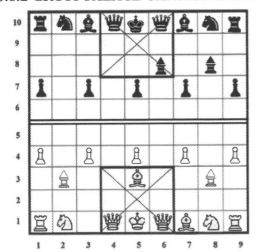

| 1 B3153 | C2868 |
| Or 1 B7153 | C8848 |

D 5.8.4 PAWN DEFENSE

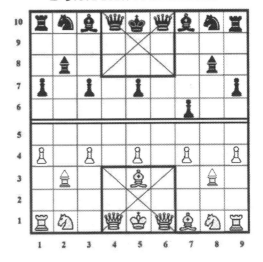

| 1 B3153 | P7776/3736 |
| Or 1 B7153 | P3736/7776 |

9.   KNIGHT OPENING

D 5.9.1 1 N2133/N8173

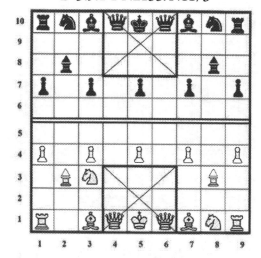

D 5.9.3 CANNON CENTER DEFENSE

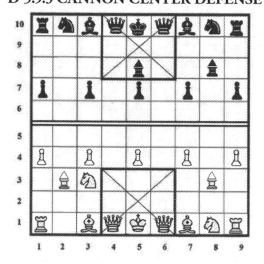

Knight Opening is a conservative opening. White wants to play safe. The following three are the popular Black's answers to Knight Opening.

1 N2133	C2858/8858
Or 1 N8173	C8858/2858

D 5.9.2 PAWN DEFENSE

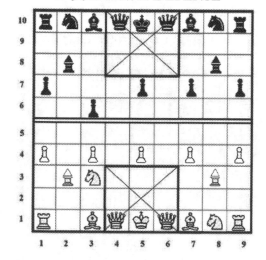

D 5.9.4 KNIGHTS GAME

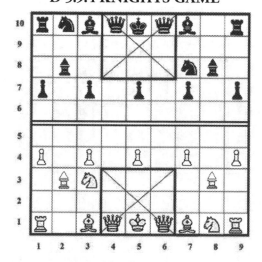

1 N2133	P3736/7776
Or 1 N8173	P7776/3736

1 N2133	N8078/N2038
Or 1 N8173	N2038/N8078

10. THE FOUR MAJOR DEFENSE SYSTEMS USING KNIGHTS AGAINST CENTER CANNON OPENING

D 5.10.1 DOUBLE-KNIGHTS DEFENSE

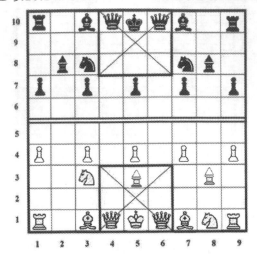

Double-Knights Defense is the most effective and popular defense system used by Black to defend the Center Cannon Opening. The characteristic of this defense is to use both Knights @38 and @78 to guard the King's Pawn @57. The following three are also the popular defensive systems against the Center Cannon Opening.

D 5.10.3 PALACE KNIGHT DEFENSE

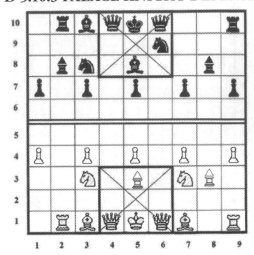

Palace Knight Defense is used by some players. The characteristic of this defense is, while one Knight is either @38 or @78, the other Knight is inside the Palace @69 or @49.

D 5.10.2 ELBOW KNIGHT DEFENSE

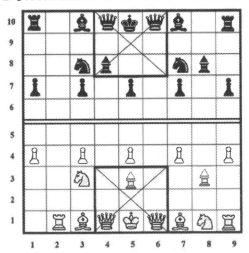

Elbow Knight Defense is frequently used and strong to defend the Center Cannon Opening. The characteristic of this defense is one Cannon placed at one of the palace corner squares (@43 or @63), between the two defending Knights @38 and @78.

D 5.10.4 SINGLE KNIGHT DEFENSE

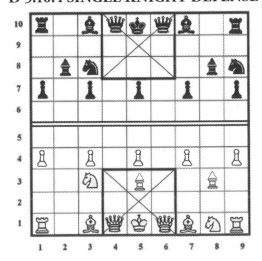

Single Knight Defense was quite popular in the past. The characteristic of this defense is only one Knight to defend the King's Pawn @57, the other Knight is put at the edged file either @18 or @98.

11. SOME POPULAR OFFENSE SYSTEMS USED TO ATTACK DOUBLE- KNIGHTS DEFENSE

D 5.11.1

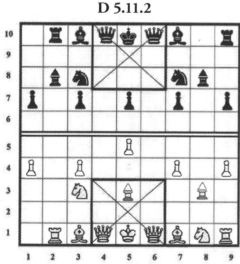

1. Filed Rook Offense

The Filed Rook Offense is an aggressive offense. One White Rook coming out early on the 2nd or 8th file, and moving to @27 or @87 is the characteristic of the offense.

D 5.11.2

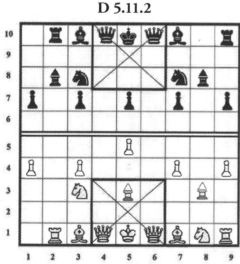

2. Central Offense

Once the King's Pawn is used, moving from @54 to @55 to attack in the middle, the "Central Offense" is called. This type of offense will result a fierce fighting in the middle files.

D 5.11.3

3. Double Cannons Offense

One Cannon, other than the one @53, places itself @52 in order to reinforce the Central Offense. The "Double Cannons Offense" is called. This opening is rare to be used.

D 5.11.4

4. 56 Cannons Offense

Once the two White Cannons, one is @53 and the other is @43 or @63, are side by side with the center Cannon @53, the "56 Cannons Offense" is called.

D 5.11.5

5. 57 Cannons Offense

One of the two White Cannons is @53, the other is either @33 or @73, in the 3rd or 7th File, in the "57 Cannons Offense".

D 5.11.7

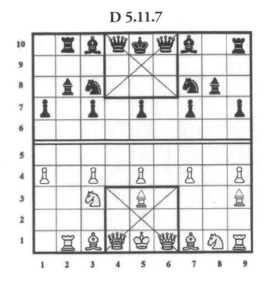

7. 59 Cannons Offense

The characteristic of "59 Cannons Offense" is: One Cannon @53, the other is on the edged file @13 or @93.

D 5.11.6

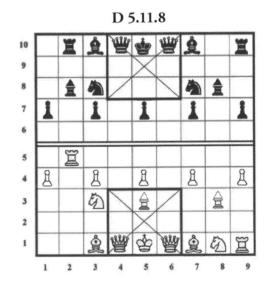

6. 58 Cannons Offense

One White Cannon is @53, and the other moves to @27 or @87 in the 2nd or 8th File, in the "58 Cannons Offense".

D 5.11.8

8. Border Rook Offense

The Border Rook Offense is a cautious offense. White places his filed Rook @25 or @85 on the border, initiate of the attack.

D 5.11.9

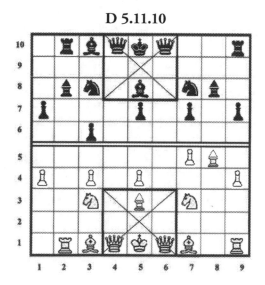

9. Knight Offense

White's Knight advances to the border from @73 to @65 and leads the attack, in the "Knight Offense".

D 5.11.10

10 Border Cannon Offense

When a White Cannon moves on the border line to @85 or @25 in the 5th Rank, the offense is called "Border Cannon Offense".

D 5.11.11

11. Two Rooks Offense

When White starts one of his Rooks in a File, and another in a Rank, it is called the "Two Rooks Offense".

D 5.11.12

12. Ranked Rook Offense

The characteristic of the "Ranked Rook Offense" is the first White Rook starts in a rank, @12 or @92.

D 5.11.13

13. Delay Rooks Offense

"Delay Rook Offense" is the offense where both White Rooks stay back in their opening positions @11 and @91, and don't want to come out early in the opening stage.

12. SOME POPULAR DOUBLE-KNIGHTS DENFENSE SYSTEMS USED TO DEFEND CENTER CANNON OPENING

D 5.12.1

D 5.12.3

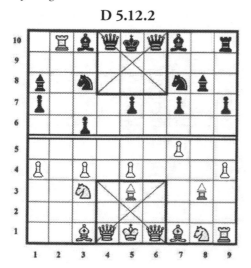

1. Rook Exchange Declined

In this case, Black moves his Cannon @28 aside and offers an exchange of the White's Filed Rook @27with his Rook @20, the White Rook rejects the offer and moves to @37. This defense is called the "Rook Exchange Declined". This is a very popular opening at all time.

3. Bishop Defense

When a Black Bishop @58 is used in the early opening phase to remove the invading enemy's Bishop Pawn @76 or @36, it is called the "Bishop Defense".

D 5.12.2

D 5.12.4

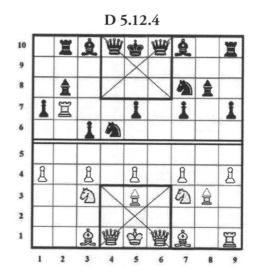

2. Rook Exchange Accepted

When the White Rook @27 takes Black's offer for a Rook exchange, as shown in D 5.12.2, this defense is called the "Rook Exchange Accepted".

4. Knight Counter Attack

Black moves his Knight from @38 to @46 to lead the counter-attack as shown in D5.12.4, the defense is called "Knight Counter Attack".

D 5.12.5

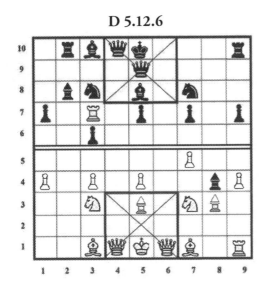

D 5.12.7

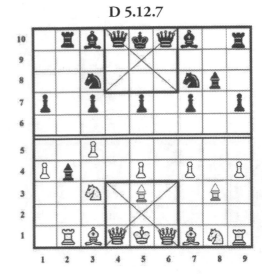

5. Palace Rook Defense

Black moves a Rook from @10 to @40, or @90 to @60, inside the Palace, the defense is called "Palace Rook Defense"

7. Cannon Blocking

Cannon Blocking is the defense where Black moves the Cannon @24 (or @84) to block the White's filed Rook @21 (or @81).

D 5.12.6

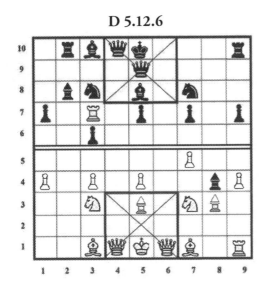

D 5.12.8

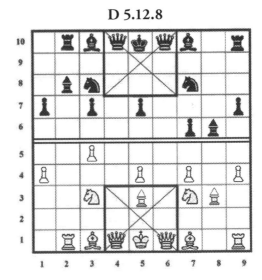

6. Knight's Gambit Accepted

When the White Rook @27 moves to catch the unprotected Knight @38, as shown in D.5.12.6, the defense is called "Knight's Gambit Accepted".

8. Cannon Border Patrol

Black uses one of his Cannons @86 or @26 on the Border to do the defense work. This is called "Cannon Border Patrol".

D 5.12.9

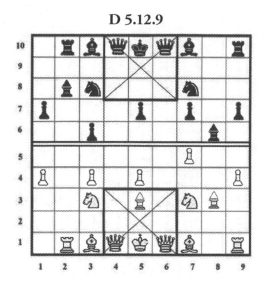

D 5.12.11

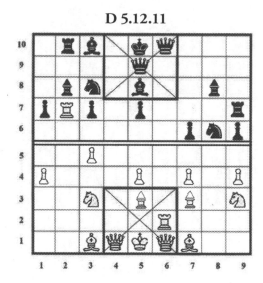

9. Cannon Border Defense

"Cannon Border Defense", as shown in D5.12.9, is different from "Cannon Border Patrol", due to the fact that the border Cannon @86 can help the Knight @38 to force the White Rook @21 to make a retreat back to @11.

11. Edged Rook Defense

A Black Rook moves up three squares along the edge file from @90 to @97, as shown in D5.12.11, to reinforce the protection of the King's Pawn @57, is an defense called the "Edged Rook Defense".

D 5.12.10

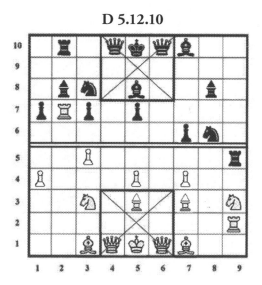

D 5.12.12

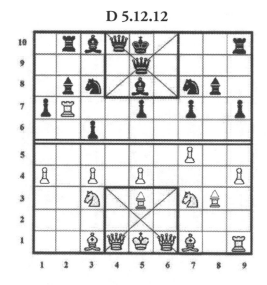

10. Edged Rook Counter Attack

A Black Rook starts its opening move up along the edge file from @90 to @95, as shown in D 5.12.10. This defense is called the "Edged Rook Counter Attack".

12. Knight's Gambit Declined

D 5.12.12 shows the White Rook @27, realizing that a gambit is set up and declines to move to @37, even the Black Knight @38 is unprotected. This is called the "Knight's Gambit Declined".

D 5.12.13

D 5.12.15

13. Rook Counter Attack

In the 3rd move of a new game, Black moves his Rook from @10 to @20 or @90 to @80 in order to control the open 2nd or 8th file. This kind of aggressive defense is called the "Rook Counter Attack".

15. Two Pawns Defense

Black develops his two Pawns from @37 to @36 and @77 to @76. It is called the "Two Pawns Defense".

D 5.12.14

14. Edged Rook Protection

A Black Rook moves up two squares along the edge file from its opening position @10 to protect the Cannon @28, as shown in D5.12.14, this defense is called the "Edged Rook Protection".

13.   CANNONS GAME

D 5.13.1 Filed Rook vs. Delay Rooks

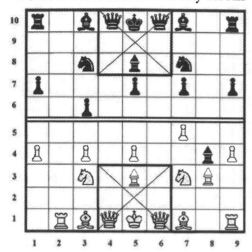

White's filed Rook comes out from @11 to @21, while the two Black Rooks are still idle. White of course gains in this opening but not too much.

D 5.13.2 Filed Rook vs. Ranked Rook

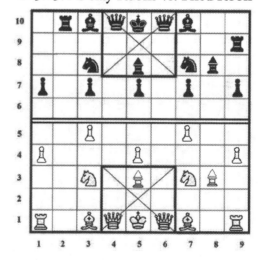

White's filed Rook moves to @21, and Black responds with a ranked Rook opening @19. This kind of opening has been popular at all time.

D 5.13.3 Ranked Rook vs. Filed Rook

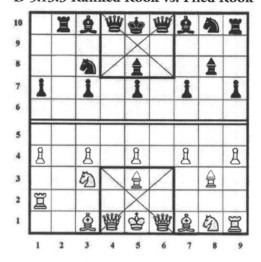

White's ranked Rook moves from @11 to @12, while Black answers with a filed Rook from @10 to @20. This opening has been popular as well.

D 5.13.4 Delay Rooks vs. Filed Rook

White at this point of opening still keeps his two Rooks ready but no actions, even the two Black's Rooks are out. A few top players do play this kind of opening.

14. CANNON COUNTER ATTACK

D 5.14.1 Filed Rook vs. Cannon Blocking

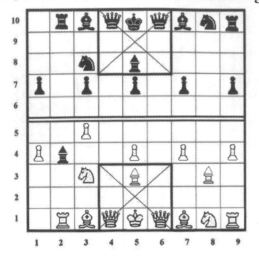

Black applies this kind of defensive opening "Cannon Blocking" moving Cannon C2824 to block the White filed Rook @21.

D 5.14.3 Filed Rook vs. Ranked Rook

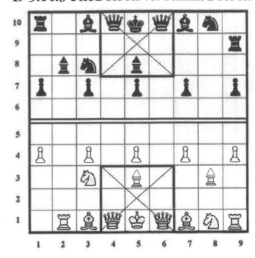

Black brings out his ranked Rook from @90 to @99 early to challenge White's filed Rook @21.

D 5.14.2 Delay Rooks vs. Filed Rook

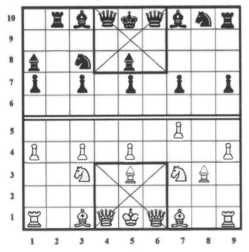

This opening is not often played. The characteristics this defense is that, there is an open file, Black starts moving a Rook out to command the open file.

D 5.14.4 Rook Exchange

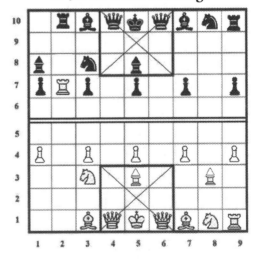

Black offers a Rook exchange at this early stage, so that Black can release the pressure from White and to simplify the game.

15. SOME PRINCIPLES OF THE OPENING

1. Don't start the game with the King's Pawn or Rook's Pawn.
2. Start with a Pawn Opening or Cannon Opening, if you are playing the aggressive White.
3. Develop the Knights and the Rooks as early as possible.
4. Protect the King's Pawn. Make sure it is adequately protected.
5. Do not move the King unless absolutely necessary.
6. Move the Pawn forward (if safe) to clear room for Knight's development.
7. Do not move the same piece more than three times during the opening phase.
8. Develop the major pieces (Rooks, Knights, Cannons) with balance so that no weakness on either flank.
9. Keep the Rooks away from any danger to avoid being a target of a trap or an attack.
10. To exchange a Knight and a Cannon with a Rook is always considered a gain in material. The Rook side should avoid that kind of exchange.
11. Try to familiarize as much as possible some of your favorite openings.
12. 12. Study and review the traps in the opening from books or personal experiences in playing.

16. SOME OPENING GUIDES

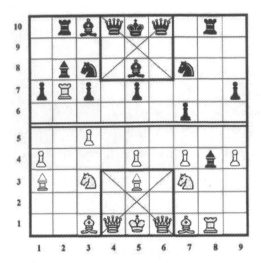

D 5.16.1

This game shows some principles of opening: 1) Start a game with a Cannon opening. 2) Start developing the Knights, then the Rooks. 3) Protect the King's Pawn. 4) Move up the Pawn to free the "obstructed" Knight behind. 5) Avoid moving a piece too often. 6) Develop all major pieces equally.

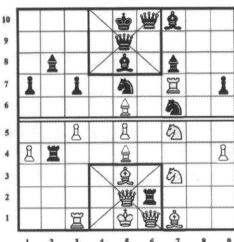

D 5.16.2

The diagram, D5.16.2, taken from a master game, indicates clearly, the importance of the middle (5th) file or the King File. All the major pieces on both sides are involved for the control of the file to get a win.

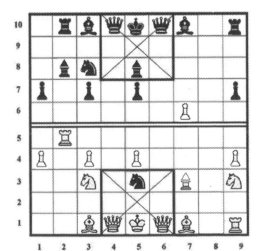

D 5.16.3

Diagram D 5.16.3 shows us that the Black Knight @53 has made four (4) moves to reach there (N8078, N7866, N6645, N4553). Black plays against one of the opening rules.

Here is the simple arithmetic to prove that:

A.   After 8 ---N4553 (after each side makes 8 moves)
B.   After 9 B7053 (after the Black Knight is taken)
 White: C1+N2+R2+P2+B1=8 moves
 Black: C1+N1+R1=3 moves.
The difference: White gains 8-(3+1) =4 moves!

17. SOME OPENING TRAPS

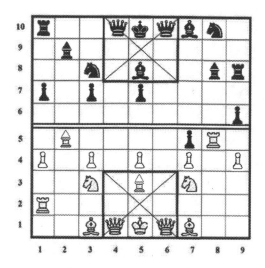

D 5.17.1 TRAP FOR THE BORDER ROOK

In this case, White's border Rook @85 is endangered by Black's troubled move of P7675, as shown in the diagram. It is a trap. If White's Pawn @74 takes the invading Pawn, then the Rook is doomed after Black's move of C2989. If Rook takes the Pawn, Black will put White's 7th File where the Rook @75, the Pawn @74, the Knight @73 and the Bishop @71 all under heavy fire by the two Black Cannons from @78 and @79. The right flank of White would be soon collapsed. If Rook retreats back to @82, White still will be in trouble after Black Pawn's move of P7574.

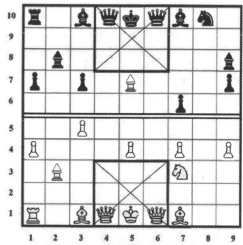

D 5.17.2 A CANNON CONTROLS THE OPEN KING FILE

If there is no piece in between the King and the King's Pawn, don't let the Pawn be taken by a Cannon. This is the worst situation for any player to have in any time of the game. D5.17.2 shows Black will have a very difficult time to get out of the deep hole.

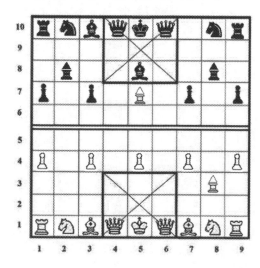

D 5.17.3 THE KING'S PAWN MAY BE POISONOUS

This is a case where the King's Pawn is unprotected, but Black has a Bishop @58 between the King and the Pawn. Most experienced players would not take the King's Pawn with the Cannon, in this early opening phase. By doing so, Black would develop his pieces faster.

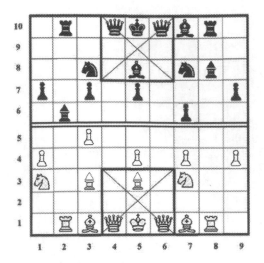

D 5.17.4 ATTEMPT TO FORCE ROOK TO RETREAT

D5.17.4 shows that Black moves the Cannon from @28 to @26 on the border line. The intention is to help the Knight @78 to develop to @86, and forces the White Rook @ 81 to retreat back to @91.

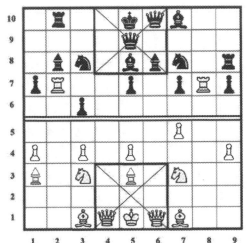

D 5.17.5 TWO TRAPPED ROOKS UNDER FIRE

In this case, the White Rook @21 makes a blunder by moving to @27. This movement puts both White Rooks @27 and @87 under attack by the Black Cannon @68, when a move of C6867 is made. White will lose a Rook.

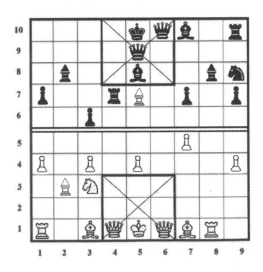

D 5.17.6 TWO ROOKS ARE IN JEOPARDY

In order to get rid of the dangerous Cannon @57, Black makes a mistake, in this case, by moving his Rook from @40 to @47, to kick the Cannon out of the square. Instead the White Cannon forks both Black's two Rooks @47 and @90 with a move of C5795! One of the Black Rooks will be taken.

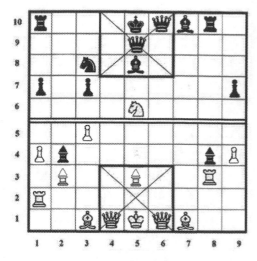

D 5.17.7 A CANNON BEHIND A KNIGHT IS DANGEROUS

This case shows that White has a complete control of the King File with a combination of a Knight and Cannon in the same file. They can cause problems with either a check of N5648+ or N5668+.

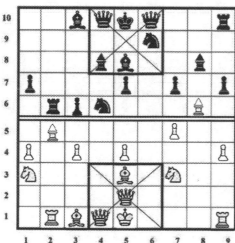

D 5.17.8 A PIN OF ROOK AND KNIGHT

Black, in this case, makes a mistake by bringing up his Knight from @38 to @46. The move provides a chance for the White Cannon @83 to make the move to C8386 and pin the Black Knight @46 and the Rook @26.

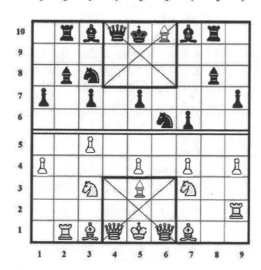

D 5.17.9 ONE QUEEN IS GAINED

Black will lose a Queen, in this case, when White's Cannon makes a move from @63 to @60, after Black moves his Knight from @78 to @66. The Knight @66 will be pinned and taken by the Rook from @92.

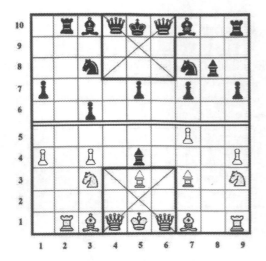

D 5.17.10 A FAILED CHECK

Black's C2454 to make a check is a mistake! In this case, the Cannon will be lost after N3354, R2021, N5433+, B7058 and N3321.

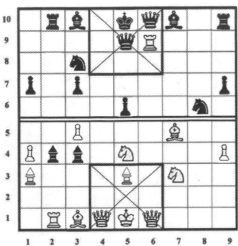

D 5.17.11 TRAP OF A CHECK

In this case, White moves his Knight from @33 to @54 to entice a check from the Black Cannon @24. It is a trap. If Black takes the Knight @54 with the Cannon, the White Cannon @53 would make a check with C5356+. This would cost Black a Cannon after a Rook exchange.

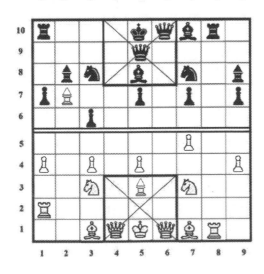

D 5.17.12 PREMATURE OF OFFER AN EXCHANGE

In this case, Black makes an offer for a Rook exchange too early with a move of C8898, without considering that the White Rook @12 will catch his trapped Knight later after a Rook exchange.

(1_ _ _C8898, 2 R8180 N7880, 3 R1282 N8078, 4 R8288 N3840, 5 C2777 R1020, 6 C7770+ B5870, 7 R8878)

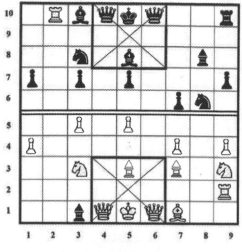

D 5.17.13 ONE BISHOP IS GAINED

In this case, Black offers a Rook exchange to gain a Bishop by moving Cannon from @24 to @34 (1___ C2434, 2 R2120 C3431+, 3 Q4152 N3820). Black gains a Bishop.

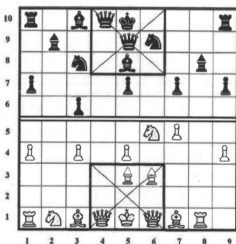

D 5.17.14 THE LOSS OF A FALSELY-PROTECTED PIECE

The diagram shows the Black Cannon @ 88 is a falsely-protected piece. Once the protector (the Black Knight @69), is removed, after the exchange (1 C6369 C2969), then the Cannon @88 will be captured by the Rook @81.

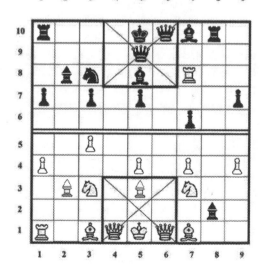

D 5.17.15 A KNIGHT'S GAMBIT

In this case, the White Rook @78 accepts the Knight's Gambit by taking the Knight @78. Black has two options to start the planned counter-attack: 1) C8882, then C8272, or 2) C2824. The trapped White Rook @78 has only one way out, the move R7877. Most players would not accept this kind of Gambit. It is too risky for White to take.

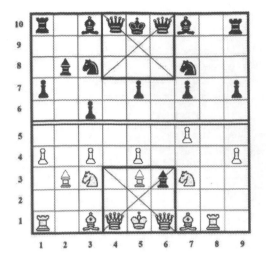

D 5.17.16 A PIN OF KNIGHT AND CANNON BY A CANNON

White makes a careless mistake, in this case, by moving his Knight from @21 to @33, and let the Black Cannon @68 to pin the knight @33 and Cannon @23 with C6863. It is a fatal mistake.

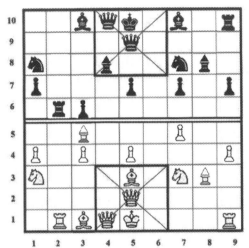

D 5.17.17 AN UNPROTECTED ROOK IS CAUGHT

The Black Rook @26 is doomed after White's tricky move C2535, the Cannon @35 threatens to mate with C3530. None of the moves P3635, B3058 or R2620 can save the Black Rook @26.

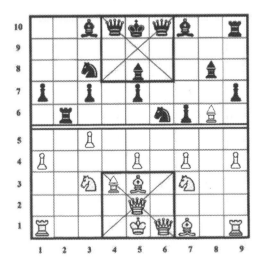

D 5.17.18 ANOTHER PIN OF ROOK AND KNIGHT

The Rook @26 and the Knight @66 are pinned by a Cannon @86. The Black Knight @66 will be captured when White makes the inevitable move of N3345.

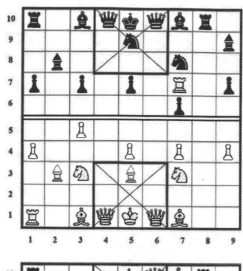

D 5.17.19 TRAP FOR A ROOK

The White Rook @77, in this case, would be trapped or in a bad situation if Black had the chance to make the move, C9979. Fortunately the Rook can make an escape by taking the Pawn @36 before it is caught.

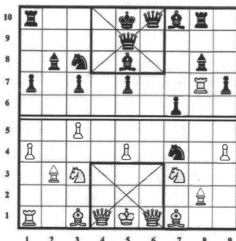

D 5.17.20 A PIN OF ROOK AND CANNON BY A ROOK

Both the unprotected Black Rook @80 and Cannon @88 are pinned by the White Rook @87. The Black Cannon @88 will be taken in this case.

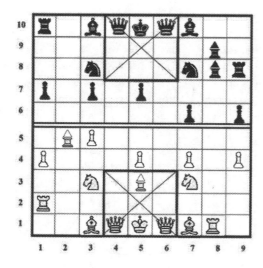

D 5.17.21 ROOK IS FORCED BACK

In this case, the White Rook @ 81 is forced to retreat back to his opening position, @91, after Black's move of C2989.

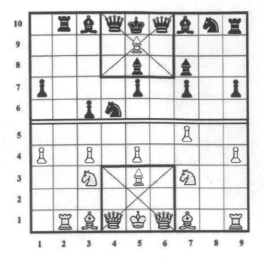

D 5.17.22 GAIN OF THE KING'S PAWN

In this case, White gains the important King's Pawn by taking the advantage of the unprotected Black Rook @20. White moves C2959 and C5957 to make a check and gains a Pawn, when both sides finish the exchange of the Rooks. (1 C2959 R2021, 2 C5957+ Q6059, 3 N3321)

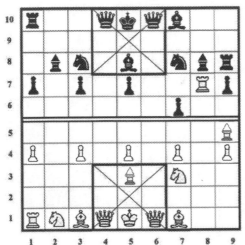

D 5.17.23 AN EDGED ROOK IS CAUGHT

The Black Rook @98 is caught by the White Cannon @95 in this case. This mistake happens if the Edged Rook side doesn't pay special attention to the movement and position of enemy's border Cannons.

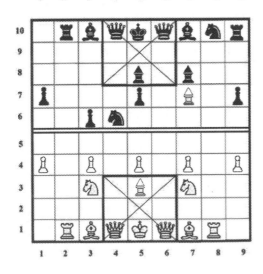

D 5.17.24 A DEADLY WEAKNESS

In this case, White alertly spots and takes the opportunity of opponent's defense weakness, and makes the winning move of C2777 to attack the Bishop @70 and makes a check, White's move would eliminate one or both Black Rooks, and of course, a final win.

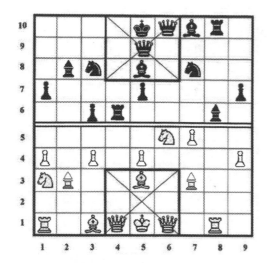

D 5.17.25 DISCOVER ATTACKS

As shown in diagram D5.17.25, the Black Rook @40 makes a move to @46, enforcing the defense. Black doesn't realize the move will cost him a major piece. Since the White Knight @77 makes a move back to @65 to attack the Rook @46, the Black Knight @78 is also under the White Cannon's fire from @73. White gains a Knight in the play.

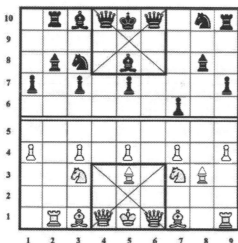

D 5.17.26 CARELESS IN OPENING

This happens often for beginners in this opening game. White takes the Knight @80 with Cannon @83. Then, the White Rook @81 will pin the Black's Rook @80 and Cannon @88.

CHAPTER 6   THE SPECIAL RULES

1.   THE DEFINITION

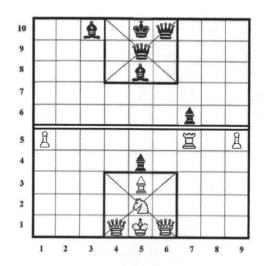

1.1 THE PROTECTED PIECE

D 6.1.1

A "Protected Piece" is a piece that is "fully", or at all the time protected by one or more pieces. A protected piece is allowed to be attacked perpetually by other hostile pieces, with exceptions: 1) A "protected Piece" is not allowed to be attacked by two or more pieces perpetually; 2) A protected Rook is not allowed to be attacked by a Knight and/or a Cannon. In D 6.1.1, the Black Cannon @76 is a protected piece and the White Rook @75 is allowed to "attack" the Cannon from making a deadly mate. In this case, Black forces for a draw by moving the Cannon onto two border squares (@76 or @36) only (other moves will result in a loss).

1.2 THE PARTLY PROTECTED PIECE

D 6.1.2

A "partly Protected Piece" is protected alternately or occasionally by a piece. A "Partly Protected Piece" is treated exactly like a "Protected Piece". In diagram D 6.1.2, the Black Cannon @96 is "partly", or alternately, protected by the Knight @77. The White Rook @85 is, therefore, allowed to "attack" the Cannon perpetually: 1 R8595 C9686, 2 R9585 C8696, _ _ _. The White Rook @85 has to do so to get a draw to save his game, since Black's C9691+ would mate: 1 --- C9691+, 2 R8581 P7161#.

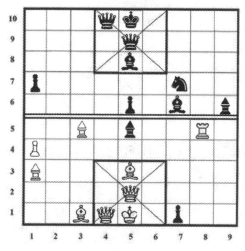

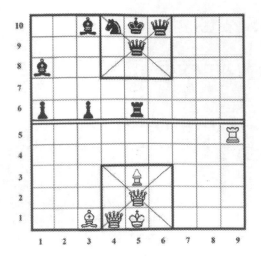

1.3 THE RESTRAINED PIECE

D 6.1.3

A "Restrained Piece" is a piece that is "restricted" in a certain square by a hostile piece, and the "Restrained Piece" has no power to protect itself or others during the period. A restrained Rook is not allowed to be attacked. In diagram D 6.1.3, the Black Rook @56 is a restrained piece. The Rook is being pinned by the White Cannon @53, and it can only move in five available squares on the King File (@54, @55, @56, @57 and @58). In this case, White Rook @95 cannot perpetually attack the restrained Black Rook, he has to stop doing that and White's hope for a draw is slim.

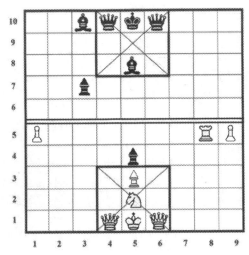

1.4 THE UNPROTECTED PIECE

D 6.1.4

An "Unprotected Piece" is a piece that has no protection from other piece. An unprotected piece is not allowed to be attacked perpetually by other piece(s) except: 1) The Kings or Pawns; 2) An unprotected piece is allowed to be attacked by a piece of the same kind; 3) A piece can attack perpetually, two unprotected pieces. In this case shown in D 6.1.4, White cannot save the game and get a draw, since his White Rook @85 is not allowed to attack the unprotected Black Cannon @37 perpetually, and hence White cannot stop the checkmate move from the Cannon.

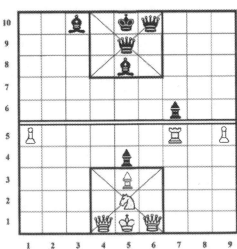

1.5 THE FALSELY PROTECTED PIECE

D 6.1.5 (Example No.1)

A "Falsely Protected Piece" is a piece that is "protected" by a piece in which the "protector" itself is either being pinned or restrained. A "Falsely Protected Piece" is treated as same as an "Unprotected Piece". In the diagram D 6.1.5, the Black Cannon @76 is a falsely protected piece (the protector Bishop @58 is pinned and restrained by White Cannon @53) and is not allowed to be attacked by the White Rook @75. White has to make changes if he doesn't want to violate the Rules, which will mean a loss for White.

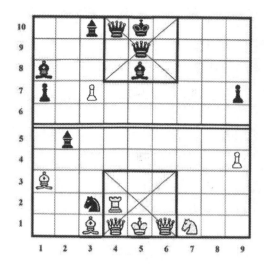

1.6 THE FALSELY PROTECTED PIECE

D 6.1.6 (Example No.2)

This is another case of the "Falsely Protected Piece". In D 6.1.6, the Black Knight @32, protected by the Cannon @30, is making a check and the White Rook @42 "stops" the check. The Black Knight @32 is, in fact, a falsely protected piece. Once the White Pawn @37 moves out of the 3rd File, the Knight will not eligible to be a falsely protected piece, and he has to escape from the White Rook's attack. In this case, Black utilizes his two Bishops to @36, teaming up with the Cannon @30, providing protecting for his Knight @32, and finally forces a draw. (1 P3747 B1836, 2 P4737 B3618, 3 P3727 B5836, 4 B1335 B3658, 5 B3553 B5836- - - -)

CHAPTER 6
THE SPECIAL RULES

1(A) THE ILLEGAL MOVE (MOVE THAT IS NOT ALLOWED TO PLAY)

1) Perpetual Check.
2) Perpetual Attack on an Unprotected Piece (Except the King or Pawns).
3) Perpetual Attack on an Unprotected Piece by a Cannon and other Movable Piece(s).
4) Perpetual Attack on a Falsely Protected Piece.
5) Perpetual Attack on a Restrained Rook by a Knight or a Cannon.
6) Perpetual Attack on a Restrained Piece by a Piece of the Same Kind.
7) Perpetual Attack on a Protected or Partly Protected Piece by Two or More Pieces.
8) Perpetual Attack on a Protected Rook by a Knight or a Cannon.
9) Perpetual Attack on a Piece by the King or a Pawn with Other Piece(s) at each move.
10) Perpetual Check vs. Other Types of Moves.

1(B) THE LEGAL MOVE (MOVE THAT IS PERMITTED TO PLAY)

1) Alternate Check.
2) Perpetual Threat to Mate.
3) Perpetual Attack on a Protected or Partly Protected Piece.
4) Perpetual Attack on an Unprotected or Falsely Protected Piece by a Piece of the Same Kind.
5) Perpetual Attack on Two Unprotected and/or Falsely Protected Pieces.
6) Perpetual Attack on an Unprotected Piece by a King or a Pawn.
7) Perpetual Attack on an Unprotected Pawn (still in its Own Territory) by a Cannon and other Movable piece(s).
8) Perpetual Refusal to Capture a Hostile Piece.
9) Perpetual Blocking, Perpetual Offer of Exchange of Pieces, or Offer of Sacrifice of Piece.
10) Both Sides Violate the Same Rule.

2. THE ILLEGAL MOVES

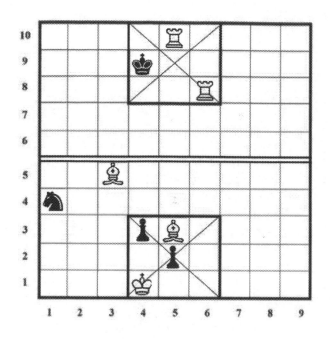

A1 PERPETUAL CHECK

D 6.2.1

1 R6869+   K4948   2 R5040+   K4858

3 R4050+   K5848   4 R6968+   K4849 - - - - -

The perpetual check is an attack to the King by a hostile piece at every single move. It is considered an illegal move in Chinese Chess. In this case, the two White Rooks @50 and @68 cannot make the perpetual check alternately.

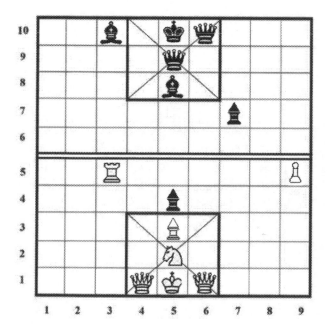

A2 PERPETUAL ATTACK ON AN UNPROTECTED PIECE

D 6.2.2

1 R3575	C7737	2 R7535	C3777
3 R3575	C7737	4 R7535	C3777 - - - - -

An unprotected piece cannot be attacked perpetually by any piece except the King or Pawns. In this case, the Black Cannon @77 is unprotected and cannot be attacked perpetually by the White Rook @35. That decision means a "Death Sentence" to White. (Without any stoppage, the Black Cannon would mate from either @71 or @31.)

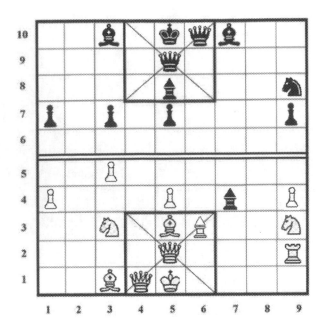

A3 PERPETUAL ATTACK ON AN UNPROTECTED PIECE BY A CANNON AND OTHER MOVABLE PIECE(S)

D 6.2.3

1 C6373	C7484	2 B5375	C8474
3 B7535	C7464	4 B9375	C6474 - - - - -

An unprotected piece is not allowed to be attacked perpetually by a Cannon and other movable piece(s). In this case, The White Cannon @63, respectively with the two Bishops @53 and @93, attack perpetually the unprotected Bishop @70. It is an illegal move, White has to make change.

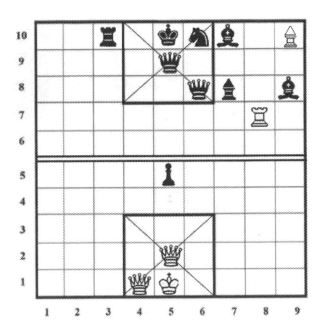

A4 PERPETUAL ATTACK ON A FALSELY PROTECTED PIECE

D 6.2.4

1 R8777	C7888	2 R7787	C8887
3 R8777	C7888	4 R7787	C8887 - - - - -

A falsely protected piece is not allowed to be attacked perpetually (same as an Unprotected piece). In this case, the Black Cannon @78 is a falsely protected piece because the protector (Knight @60) is being pinned by the White Cannon @90 and it becomes a restrained piece. White Rook is prohibited to attack the Cannon.

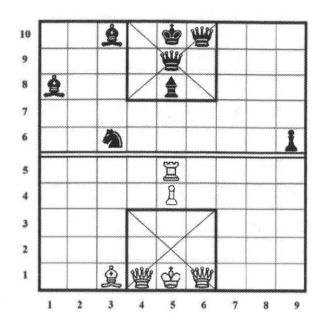

A5 PERPETUAL ATTACK ON A RESTRAINED ROOK BY A KNIGHT OR A CANNON

D 6.2.5 (CASE A) (BY KNIGHT)

1 R5556	N3648	2 R5655	N4836
3 R5556	N3644	4 R5655	N4436 - - - - -

A restrained Rook is not allowed to be attacked perpetually by a Knight and/or a Cannon. The diagram shows a Black Knight @36 is in violation of attacking the restrained Rook @55 perpetually and illegally. White has to stop attacking the Black Rook.

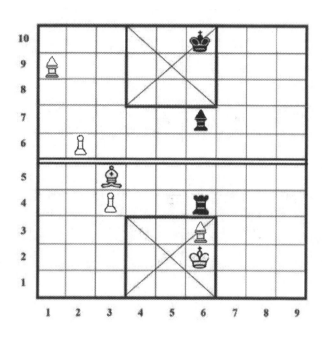

D 6.2.6 (CASE B) (BY CANNON)

1 C1914	R6465	2 C1415	R6566
3 C1516	R6664	4 C1614	R6465 - - - - -

A restrained Rook cannot be attacked by a Cannon perpetually. In this case, the White Cannon @19 is attacking the restrained Rook @64 illegally.

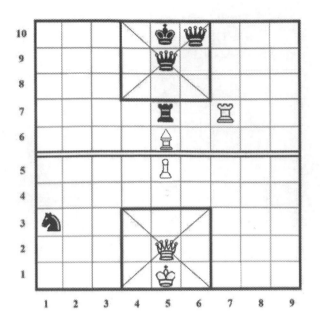

A6 THE PERPETUAL ATTACK ON A RESTRAINED PIECE BY A PIECE OF THE SAME KIND

D 6.2.7 (CASE A) (BY ROOK)

1 _ _ _   R5758   2 R7778   R5857   3 R7877 - - - - -

IN this case, The Black Rook @57 is a restrained Rook and it is illegal to be attacked by the White Rook @77 perpetually. The Black Rook has no other choice except moving between the two squares @57 and @58. Black would lose the game if he exchanges his Rook with the Cannon @56.

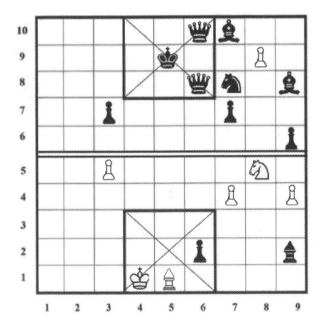

D 6.2.8 (CASE B) (BY KNIGHT)

1 N8566   N7889   2 N6685   N9778 - - - - -

The Black Knight @78 shown in D 6.2.8 is a restrained Knight and is illegally being attacked perpetually by a piece of the same kind @85. The Black Knight is obstructed by the Pawns @77 and @96 and is unable to fight back the White Knight; and if it moves to squares other than @97 and @78, it would be captured.

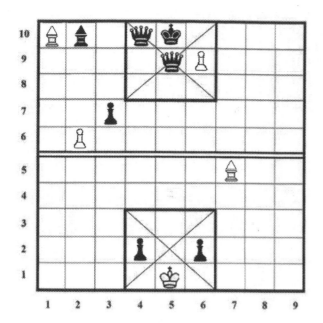

D 6.2.9 (CASE C) (BY CANNON)

1 C7525   C2030   2 C2535   C3020 - - - - -

The Black Cannon @20 is a restrained Cannon. It is being pinned by the Cannon. It is being pinned by the Cannon @10 and attacked perpetually by another White Cannon @75. It is an illegal move by a Cannon to attack the other "Restrained" Cannon perpetually

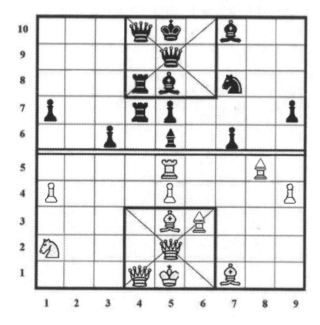

A7   PERPETUAL ATTACK ON A PROTECTED OR PARTLY PROTECTED PIECE BY TWO OR MORE PIECES

D 6.2.10

1 C8587   R4742   2 C8782   R4244

3 C6364   R4447   4 C8287   R4742 - - - - -

A protected or partly protected piece is not allowed to be attacked by two or more pieces. In this case, the two White Cannons @85 and @63 cannot perpetually attack the protected Rook @47.

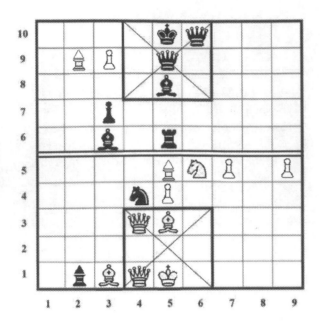

A8 PERPETUAL ATTACK ON A PROTECTED ROOK BY A KNIGHT OR A CANNON

D 6.2.11 (CASE A) (BY KNIGHT)

| 1 N6577 | R5657 | 2 N7769 | R5756 |
| 3 N6977 | R5657 | 4 N7765 | R5756 - - - - - |

A Protected Rook cannot be attacked by a Knight perpetually. In this case, the Black Rook @56 is protected by the Knight @44, and the White Knight @65 is not allowed to attack the Rook perpetually.

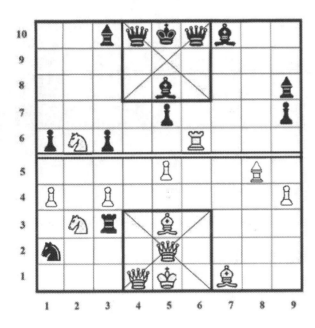

D 6.2.12 (CASE B) (BY CANNON)

| 1 C8583 | R3332 | 2 C8382 | R3233 |
| 3 C8283 | R3332 | 4 C8382 | R3233 - - - - - |

A protected Rook cannot be attacked by a Cannon either. Here in D 6.2.12, the White Cannon @85 is not allowed to attack the Black Rook @33 perpetually.

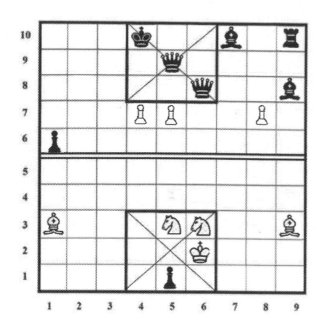

A9 PERPETUAL ATTACK ON A PIECE BY A KING OR PAWN WITH OTHER PIECES AT EACH MOVE

D 6.2.13 (CASE A) (BY KING)

1 K6252	P5161	2 K5262	P6151
3 K6252	P5161	4 K5262	P6151 - - - - -

The King @62, teams up with the two White Knights respectively @53 and @63, attack the Black Pawn @51 at every move which is illegal.

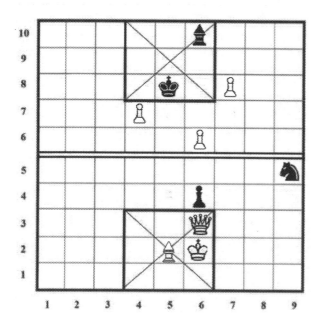

A10 PERPETUAL CHECK vs. OTHER TYPES OF MOVES

D 6.2.14 (CASE 1) (vs. ALTERNATE CHECK)

1 P6656+	P6454+	2 P5666+	P5464
3 P6656+	P6454+	4 P5666+	P5464 - - - - -

This is a very special case involving a perpetual check and a perpetual alternate check. In D 6.2.14, White makes a perpetual check which is a violation and illegal, and Black merely makes a perpetual alternate-check which is allowed. White has to stop the perpetual check on Black.

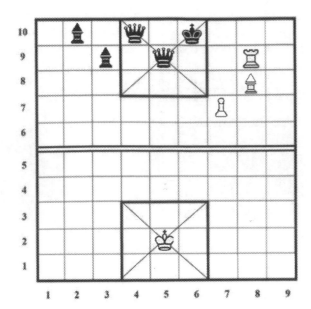

D 6.2.15 (CASE 2) (vs. PERPETUAL ATTACK)

1 R8980+	K6069	2 R8089+	K6960
3 R8980+	K6069	4 R8089+	K6960 - - - - -

This is another rare case on perpetual check. White makes the perpetual check which is an illegal move; and Black makes a perpetual attack which is not allowed as well. Since White commits a more serious violation, he is guilty. White has to make change of his next moves.

3.   THE LEGAL MOVES

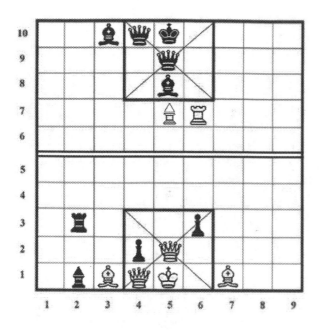

B1   ALTERNATE CHECK

D 6.3.1

1 R6787	K5060	2 R8767+	K6050
3 R6787	K5060	4 R8767+	K6050- - - - -

An "Alternate Check" is a check that is made at every two moves (alternately), which is allowed. In this case, White has to make the alternate check to get a draw with the Threefold Repetition Rule, in order to save the game.

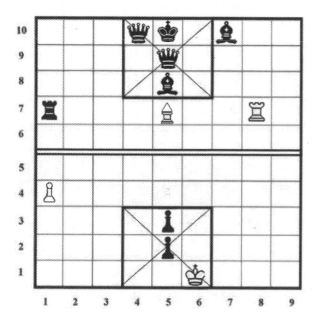

B2   PERPETUAL THREAT TO MATE

D 6.3.2

1 R8777	B7098	2 R7787	B9870
3 R8777	B7098	4 R7787	B9870 - - - - -

A perpetual threat to mate is permissible. In this case, the White Rook @87 is making the threat for a mate to get a draw to save the game from a loss. White Rook cannot move to square @67, Black has the move of P5363! White would be defeated. (1 R8767 P5363, 2 R6763 R1757>>)

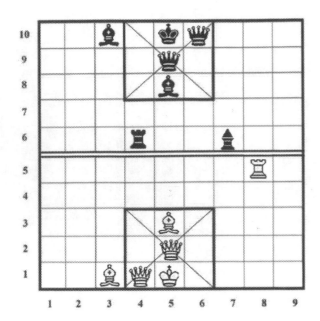

B3 PERPETUAL ATTACK ON A PROTECTED OR PARTLY-PROTECTED PIECE

D 6.3.3

1 R8575	C7656	2 R7555	C5676
3 R5575	C7656	4 R7555	C 5676- - - - -

A protected or partly protected piece can be attacked by any single piece, except, a protected Rook cannot be attacked by a Knight and/or a Cannon. In this case, the White Cannon @76 is a protected piece. There is a slim chance for Black to win in the end-game. White's best choice to get a draw is to get the Cannon in an exchange. A Rook cannot beat an experienced player with a complete Defense Unit (two Queens and two Bishops). (Chapter 4)

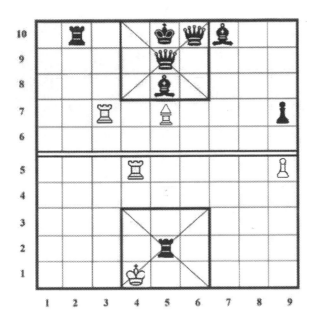

B4 PERPETUAL ATTACK ON AN UNPROTECTED OR FALSELY PROTECTED PIECE BY A PIECE OF THE SAME KIND

D 6.3.4

1 R3727	R2010	2 R2717	R1020
3 R1727	R1030	4 R2737	R3020 - - - - -

A perpetual attack on an unprotected or falsely protected piece by a piece of the same kind is allowed. In this case, the White Rook @37 is allowed to attack the unprotected Rook @20 perpetually.

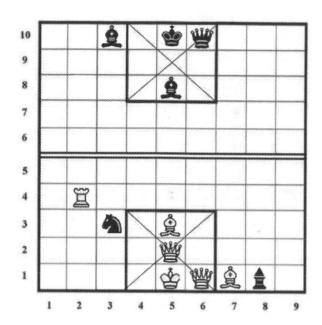

B5 PERPETUAL ATTACK ON TWO UNPROTECTED AND/OR FALSELY PROTECTED PIECES

D 6.3.5

| 1 R2434 | N3312 | 2 R3484 | C8191 |
| 3 R8414 | N1233 | 4 R1434 | N3312 - - - - - |

It is allowed for a piece to attack perpetually two unprotected and/or falsely protected pieces. In this case, the White Rook @24 is doing that to the Black Knight @33 and the Cannon @81. White will be happy with a draw.

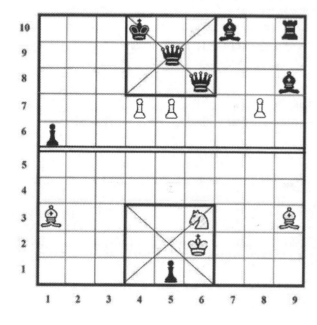

B6 PERPETUAL ATTACK ON AN UNPROTECTED PIECE BY A KING OR A PAWN

D 6.3.6 (CASE A) (BY A KING)

| 1 K6252 | P5161 | 2 K5262 | P6151 |
| 3 K6252 | P5161 | 4 K5262 | P6151 - - - - - |

The King can attack an unprotected piece perpetually. The King is also allowed to team with other piece(s) to attack an unprotected piece perpetually. In this case, the White King @62, working together with the Knight @63 alternately, attacks the Black Pawn @51. White takes the advantage of the rules and hopes to get a draw.

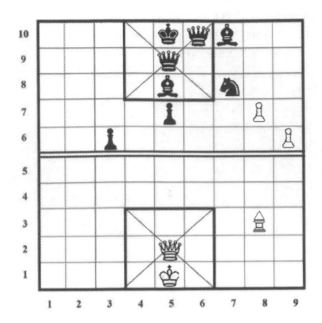

D 6.3.7 (CASE B) (BY A PAWN)

1 P8777	N7880	2 P7787	N8078
3 P8777	N7880	4 P7787	N8078 - - - - -

A Pawn alone, or together with other piece(s) alternately, is allowed to attack an unprotected piece perpetually. In this case, the White Pawn @87, together with the Cannon @83, can attack the unprotected Black Knight @78 perpetually. White is working for a drawn game by doing so.

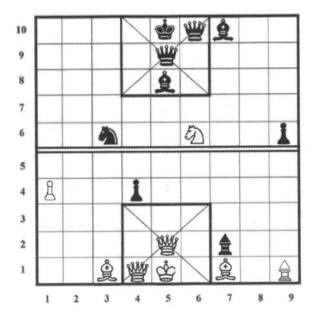

B7 PERPETUAL ATTACK ON AN UNPROTECTED PAWN STILL IN OWN TERRITORY BY A CANNON AND OTHER MOVABLE PIECE(S)

D 6.3.8

1 B7193	C7292	2 B9375	C9272
3 B7593	C7292	4 B9375	C9272 - - - - -

This is a rare case, but the readers have to know it. Prior to crossing the border, a Pawn can be perpetually attacked legally by a combination of a Cannon and a piece. The Black Pawn @96 is allowed to be attacked perpetually by the White Cannon @91 and another piece, the Bishop @71. White is looking for a draw.

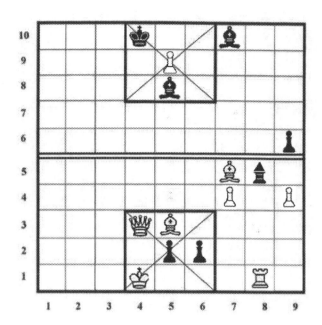

B8 PERPETUAL REFUSAL TO CAPTURE A HOSTILE PIECE

D 6.3.9

1 R8182	C8584	2 R8281	C8485
3 R8182	C8584	4 R8281	C8485 - - - - -

This is considered, undoubtedly, a very strange case. As shown in D 6.3.9, the White Rook @81 refuses to capture the unprotected Black Cannon @85 perpetually. This move is considered legal. It is automatically a draw if a legal move with a "Threefold Repetition" is made, that is a game that both sides cannot win. (If 1 R8185 P6261, 2 R8581 P6151+, 3 R8151 P5251+, 4 K4151=). And both sides are willing to settle the game with a draw.

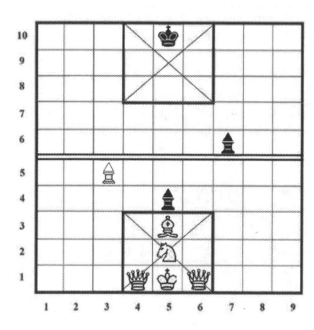

B9 PERPETUAL BLOCKING, PERPETUAL OFFER OF EXCHANGE OF PIECES, OR OFFER OF SACRIFICE OF PIECE

D 6.3.10 (CASE A) (PERPETUAL BLOCKING)

1 C3575	C7636	2 C7535	C3686
3 C3585	C8696	4 C8595	C9686 - - - - -

A "Perpetual Block" is allowed. As shown, the White Cannon @35 is perpetually blocking the Black Cannon @76 from making a mate. (If 2- - -C3686, 3 C3575 C8681+ 4 C3531 K5059#).

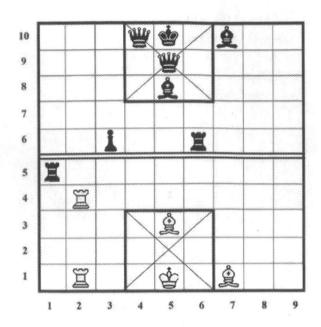

D 6.3.11 (CASE B) (PERPETUAL OFFER OF EXCHANGE OF PIECES)

1 R2425	R1517	2 R2527	R1715
3 R2725	R1517	4 R2527	R1714 - - - - -

Perpetual "Offer of Exchange of Pieces of the Same Kind" is allowed. In this case, the White Rook @24 is offering an exchange with the Black Rook @15, preventing the deadly move of the Black Rook @15 to the 6th file. White wants a drawn game.

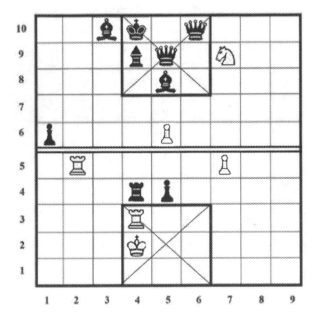

D 6.3.12 (CASE C) (PERPETUAL OFFER OF SACRIFICE OF PIECE)

1 R2524	R4445	2 R2425	R4544
3 R2524	R4447	4 R2427	R4744 - - - - -

This is an interesting case. The White Rook @43 is pinned by the Cannon @49. The other White Rook @25 is trying to make a sacrifice to save the other Rook @43 from C4943. The Black Rook @44 refuses to accept the offer because White would win the game if the "offer" is accepted (- - -R4424+, R4349#). The Rule says: "A perpetual offer of sacrifice of piece is allowed". White in this case forces the game a draw.

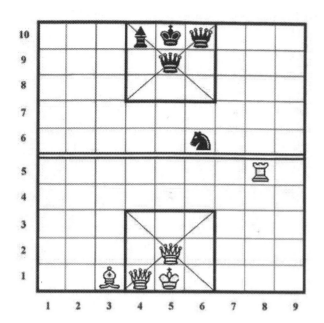

B10 BOTH SIDES VIOLATE THE SAME RULE

D 6.3.13 (CASE 1) (PERPETUAL ATTACK ON UNPROTECTED PIECE)

1 R8586	N6674	2 R8676	N7455
3 R7675	N5567	4 R7576	N6746 - - - - -

This is a special case involving two different kinds of pieces that are attacking each other perpetually. This is a draw because both sides violate the same rule simultaneously: "Attack an unprotected piece perpetually". The diagram shows exactly that the Black Knight @66 and the White Rook @85 are attacking each other perpetually. Both sides do not want to take risk in this case.

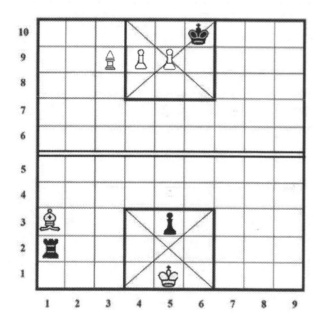

D 6.3.14 (CASE 2) (PERPETUAL THREAT TO MATE)

1 P5969+	K6050	2 K5161	P5363
3 P6959+	K5060	4 K6151	P6353 - - - - -

This is a funny case. Both sides are threatening to mate in next move: White with P6960 or Black with R1211. Both sides are afraid of losing and do not want to make changes. It is a draw.

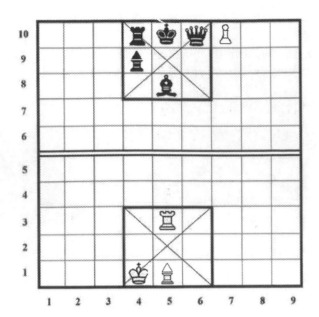

D 6.3.15 (CASE 3) (PERPETUAL CHECK)

1 R5358+   C4959+   2 R5848+   C5949+

3 R4858+   C4959+   4 R5848+   C5949+ - - - - -

This is a rare case. Both sides are making the perpetual check simultaneously. A perpetual check is definitely an illegal move in Chinese Chess. This happens on both sides. It is a draw. The White Rook @54 makes a check move with R5358, Black Cannon @49 responds with a discover-check C4959, and so on.

4. SOME STUDY CASES OF THE SPECIAL RULES

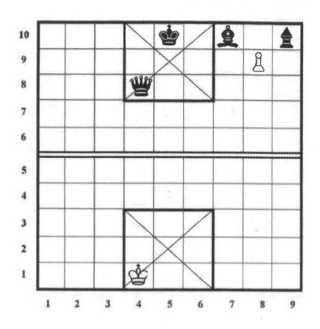

D 6.4.1 CASE 1

1 P8999	C9080	2 P9989	C8090
3 P8999	C9080	4 P9989	C8090- - - - -

The White Pawn @89 can attack perpetually an unprotected piece (the Black Cannon @90). White tries to get a draw. (See B6)

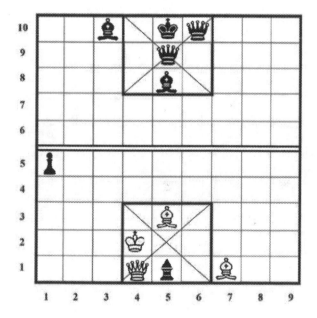

D 6.4.2 CASE 2

1 K4252	C5161	2 K5262	C6151
3 K6252	C5161	4 K5262	C6151 - - - - -

The White King @42 is allowed to attack perpetually an unprotected piece (the Black Cannon @51 in this case). Only the Kings and Pawns have this kind of privilege (allow to attack the unprotected pieces). White forces a draw. (See B6)

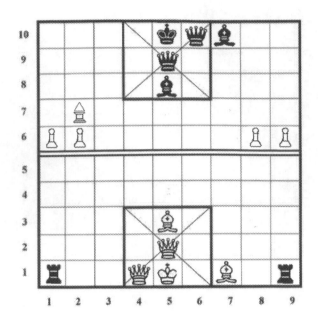

D 6.4.3 CASE 3

1 C2717	R1121	2 C1797	R9181
3 C9727	R2111	4 C2787	R8191 - - - - -

The perpetual attack on two unprotected pieces by a piece is allowed. This is exactly the case, where the White Cannon @27 is attacking respectively and perpetually the two Rooks @11 and @91. White is likely to get a draw. (See B5)

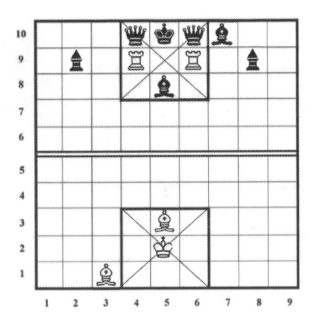

D 6.4.4 CASE 4

1 R6967	Q4059	2 R6769	Q5940
3 R4945	Q4059	4 R4549	Q5940 - - - - -

This is an unusual case. The White's two Rooks and Black's two Cannons are attacking each other perpetually. Both violate the same rule. White is aware that "One Rook alone cannot win over two Queens and two Bishops". So instead of wiping out the two Cannons with a Rook, White prefers to settle the game with a draw. (See B10)

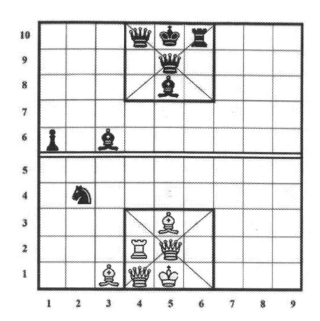

D 6.4.5 CASE 5

1 R4244	N2432+	2 R4442	N3224

3 R4244	N2432+	4 R4442	N3224 - - - - -

In this case, the White Rook @42 attacks perpetually the unprotected Black Knight @24, and it is an illegal move. The Knight @24 attacks the Rook alternately which is legal and allowed. White must make the changes. White has to accept the loss of the game. (See A2)

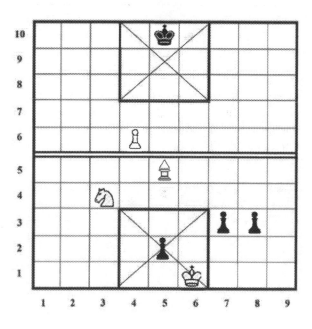

D 6.4.6 CASE 6

1 N3453	P5242	2 N5334	P4252

3 N3453	P5242	4 N5334	P4252 - - - - -

An unprotected piece cannot be attacked perpetually by any piece, except the King or Pawn. In this case, the White Knight @34 violates this rule by attacking the unprotected Pawn @52 perpetually and has to change his moves. White tries to save a defeat. (See A2)

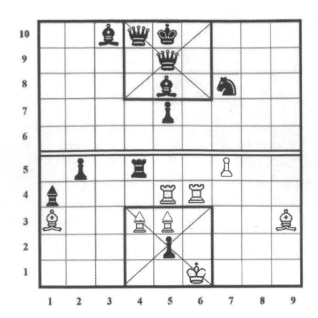

D 6.4.7 CASE 7

1 R5444	R4555	2 R4454	R5545
3 R5444	R4555	4 R4454	R5545 - - - - -

There is a special illegal rule on the unprotected piece issue which states that "The perpetual attack on an unprotected piece by a Cannon and a movable piece is illegal". In this case, the White Rook @54 and the Cannons @53 and @43 are violating this special rule, since the Black Rook @45 is an unprotected piece. White has to stop the attack. (See A3) (White is in trouble)

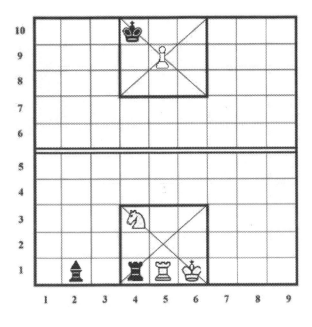

D 6.4.8 CASE 8

1 N4322	R4131	2 N2243	R3141
3 N4322	R4131	4 N2243	R3141 - - - - -

The White Rook @51 is a restrained piece in this case, and being pinned by the Cannon @21. The Black Rook @41 is not restrained but an unprotected piece, and can be attacked perpetually by a Rook (a piece of the same kind), but not a Knight or a Cannon. Black realizes he would lose the game if he makes any change in this situation. White must stop the attack on the Black Rook. (See A2)

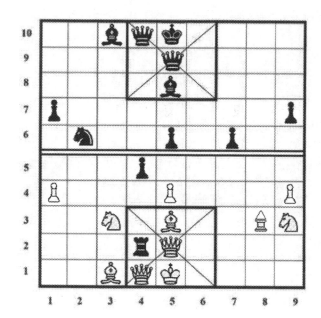

D 6.4.9 CASE 9

1 C8382	R4244	2 C8284	R4442
3 C8482	R4244	4 C8284	R4442- - - - -

The Black Rook @42 in this case is unprotected. The White Cannon @83 cannot attack the Rook perpetually. It is an illegal move. White must make the changes. (See A2)

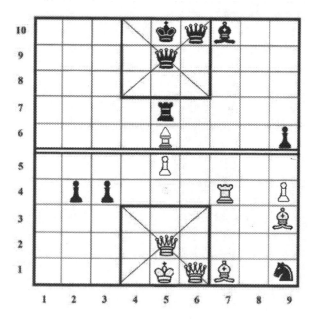

D 6.4.10 CASE 10

1 R7477	R5758	2 R7778	R5857
3 R7877	R5758	4 R7778	R5857- - - - -_

A partly protected piece is treated as same as a protected piece. Protected Rook can be attacked perpetually by other pieces, except the Knight or Cannon. In this case, the Black Rook @57 is partly protected by the Bishop @70, though it is also a restrained piece. The White Rook @74 is, therefore, allowed to attack perpetually the partly protected Rook @57. (See B3)

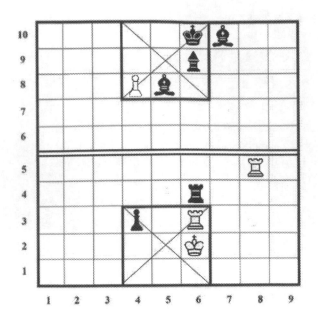

D 6.4.11 CASE 11

1 R8584	R6465	2 R8485	R6564
3 R8584	R6466	4 R8486	R6664 - - - - -

This is an unprotected Rook that can be attacked perpetually by a hostile Rook (but not a Knight or a Cannon). The Black Rook @64 is not a restrained Rook and therefore it can be attacked perpetually by the White Rook @85. The game should be a draw if no changes are made. (See B4)

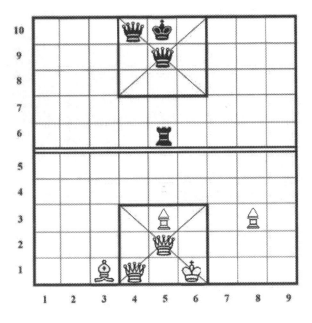

D 6.4.12 CASE 12

1 C8384	R5654	2 C8487	R5457
3 C8786	R5756	4 C8684	R5654 - - - - -

In this case, the restrained Black Rook @56 can move up and down the 5th File to "block" the Cannon @83 from White's right flank to left to make a checkmate. Black makes no violation of any rule. It is a pure blocking move and a draw.(See B9)

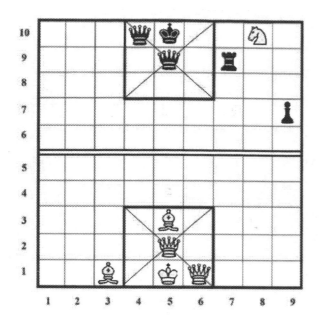

D 6.4.13 CASE 13

1 N8098	R7978	2 N9880	R7879
3 N8098	R7978	4 N9880	R7879 - - - - -

In this case, the White Knight @80 attacks the Black Rook @79 perpetually, and is illegal and not permissible. On the other hand, the Black Rook only makes the alternating check to the Knight and has no violation of the rules. Hence, White must make the changes. Even it will mean a loss to White. (SeeA2)

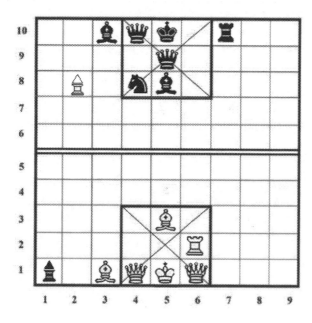

D 6.4.14 CASE 14

1 R6212	C1121	2 R1222	C2111
3 R2212	C1121	4 R1222	C2111 - - - - -

The Black Cannon @11 is unprotected in this case. The White Rook @62 cannot attack perpetually the unprotected Cannon. It is illegal and White has to stop the attacking. (See A2)

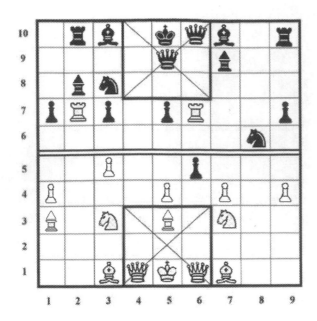

D 6.4.15 CASE 15

1	R6777	N8678	2	R7767	N7886
3	R6777	N8678	4	R7767	N7886 - - - - -

This kind of case happens in the opening phase. The unprotected White Rook @67, under attack by the Knight @86, moves to @77 to attack the Black Cannon @79. Then the Black Knight comes back from @86 to @78 and attacks the Rook with the Cannon. Black makes the perpetual attack and White only makes the alternate attack. Black has to make changes. (See A2)

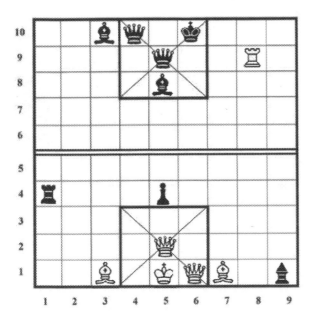

D 6.4.16 CASE 16

1	R8980+	K6069	2	R8081	C9196
3	R8189+	K6960	4	R8986	C9691 - - - - -

A perpetual alternate check is allowed and legal. In this case, White takes the advantage of this rule to obtain a draw by the rule of "Threefold Repetition". White Rook @89 is making an allowed alternate check. (See B1)

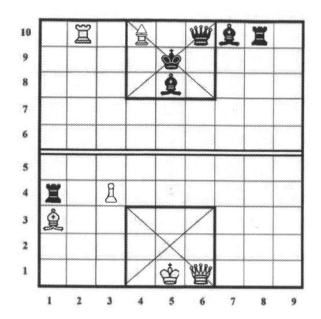

D 6.4.17 CASE 17

1 R2029+	K5950	2 R2920	K5059
R 2029+	K5950	4 R2920	K5059 - - - - -

This case has no violation of the rules. The diagram indicates white is a Rook down and eager to get back even or settle with a draw. White is fortunate in this case to be able to achieve his goal. White Rook @20 is making an alternate check; and when the King is at @50, the Rook and the Cannon @40 threaten to make a discover check with a move of C4060 to capture the Black Rook @80 or C4044 to get the Rook @14. Black prefers to settle with a draw. (See B2)

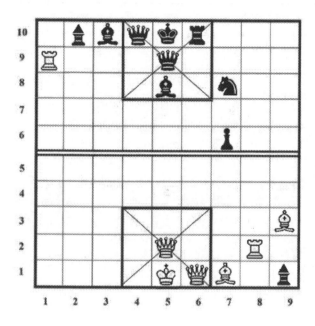

D 6.4.18 CASE 18

1 R1929	C2010	2 R8292	C9181
3 R2919	C1020	4 R9282	C8191 - - - - -

A perpetual attack on two unprotected pieces is permissible. White is in trouble and needs a draw badly in this case. The two Black Cannons @20 and @91 are unprotected. The two White Rooks attacking the two unprotected Cannons is, therefore, allowed. (See B5)

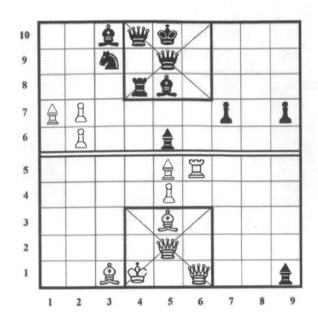

D 6.4.19 CASE 19

1 C1716	C5657	2 C1617	C5756
3 C1716	C5657	4 C1617	C5756 - - - - -

A perpetual attack on an unprotected piece by a piece of the same kind is permissible. In this case, White is a major piece down and is happy to settle with a draw. The Cannon @17 is, therefore, allowed to perpetual attack the unprotected Black Cannon @56. (See B4)

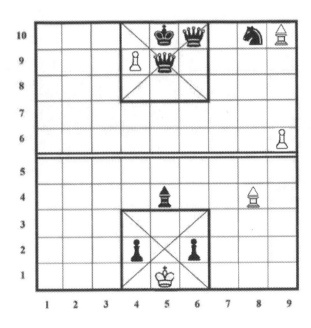

D 6.4.20 CASE 20

1 P9686	C5585	2 P8676	C8575
3 P7686	C7585	4 P8676	C8575 - - - - -

In this case, the Black Knight @80 is a piece restrained and unprotected. The White Cannon @84 and a movable Pawn @96, teaming up together to attack the Black Knight @80 perpetually and have to be stopped due to illegality. White must make the changes. (See A3)

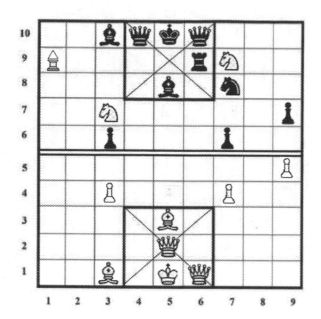

D 6.4.21 CASE 21

1 N3749   Q6059   2 N4937   Q5960

3 N3729   Q6059   4 N2937   Q5960- - - - -

The perpetual attack on a restrained Rook by a Knight and /or a Cannon is illegal. In this case, the Black Rook @69 is not restrained or pinned by the Knight @79, which the Rook can easily get rid of. However, when the White Cannon @19 and the Knight @37 act together to attack the Black Rook perpetually, White commits a violation of the specific said rule in this case. White must make changes. (See A5)

CHAPTER 7   THE MIDDLE GAME

1.   THE PRINCIPLES OF THE MID-GAME

1.1 BE PHYSICALLY AND MENTALLY PREPARED

* Sleep well, eat well and rest well.
* Getting up early. Don't be late for the game.
* Don't be nervous and relax. Keep reminding yourself it is just a game.
* Have self-confidence and believe you can win the game.
* Never under-estimate your opponent and play your game carefully and cautiously.
* Think before you touch the piece and do not rush to make moves.
* Concentrate on your game. Don't get distracted or annoyed from anything during the game.
* Keep cool and patient. Wait for your chance. Everyone makes mistakes, including your opponent.

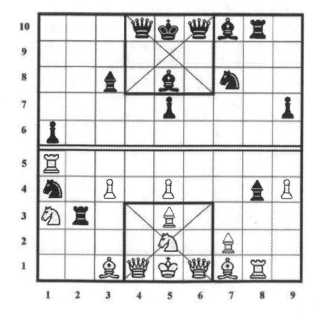

1.2 FIND THE PURPOSE OF EACH MOVE

D 7.1.1

The two most important principles of any chess games are: What is the purpose of your opponent's move? What is my correct response? Chess is a human mind game with a lot of tricks. In this case, Black advances his edged Pawn with a move P1716 to attack the White Rook @15, instead of protecting the Black Knight @14 with a rescue move R2324 from the Rook @23. Remember, don't under-estimate your opponent. It may be a mistake, it may not be! Facing this unexpected move, you should ask yourself: What is the purpose of the move?

181

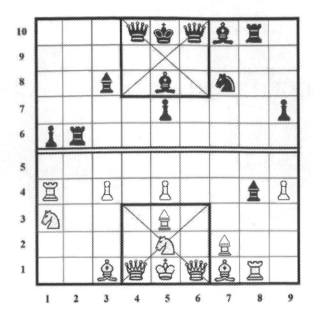

1.3 EVALUATE THE SITUATION

D 7.1.2

Using the example shown, Black tries to set up a subtle trap for the White Rook @15! If the White Rook took the Knight @14, as shown in D7.1.2, Black would move his Rook to @26 to protect the Pawn @16 and trap the Black Rook @14. The Black Rook would find no place to escape when Black brought the Cannon C3818 to attack it! The right move for White is to take the suicidal Pawn @16. This case teaches us: Don't rush, take your time to figure out and evaluate the situation carefully.

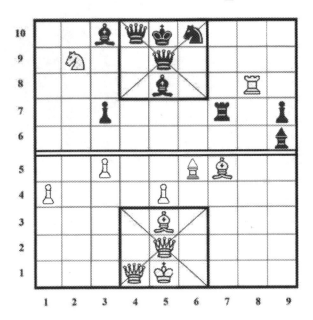

1.4 ARE YOU IN SUPERIOR SIDE?

D 7.1.3

This diagram shows that White is one Pawn ahead and his major pieces are in better positions than his counterpart. That means White has two significant mechanisms for determining who is in superior or inferior: (1) A gain in material, and (2) superior in mobility. A "gain in material" means the total sum of values of your pieces is greater than your opponent; and "superior in mobility" means your major pieces are in better positions or squares than your enemy, that enable them to have more movement room and control more squares than your adversary.

1.5 SPOT THE WEAKNESS

The following are some of the weaknesses shown in the middle game. These weaknesses can be on both sides and are targets of attacks, traps, capture or even a checkmate:

O Rooks positioned in dangerous places are subject to be the easy target for traps and attacks.

O A lone piece ventures too deep inside enemy territory without adequate friendly support.

O The protection of the King's Pawn and the center King File (the 5th File) are weak.

O King comes out of his own square (@51 for White and @50 for Black), and the King is exposed without proper protection.

O The six major pieces (Rooks, Knights and Cannons) are not evenly developed, and one flank is too weak, defensively.

O Defense Unit (2 Queens and 2 Bishops) is undermined (missing one or more pieces).

O Defense Unit is not in a better formation (the Queens and Bishops are not in their ideal defensive positions).

O Don't under-evaluate the Pawns. Whenever possible, wipe out the enemy's Pawns and advance your own Pawns.

O Rook is in a situation that it is vulnerable to a trade with a Knight and a Cannon (or two Knights, or two Cannons). Such exchange is considered a gain in material not on the Rook side, but on the other side.

O Knights or Cannons are vulnerable to be attacked or captured, if not properly protected.

O King might be in a vulnerable situation for an attack and even a mate. Don't miss the chance.

O There will be an advantage to gain if you make a specific move of piece exchange or sacrifice.

O Your adversary shows signs of impatience, annoyance, tiredness, nervousness, distraction, etc.

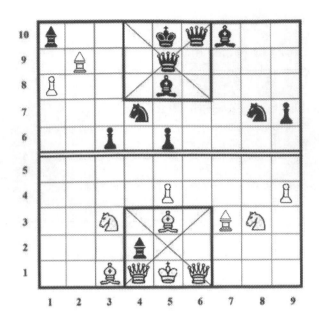

1.6 DECIDE THE RIGHT STRATEGY AND TARGET

D 7.1.4

The diagram shown was played by two great champions of Chinese Chess in 1980. White had a slim advantage in mobility, but not in material. White picked the wrong target (the Black King) in lieu of the unprotected Cannon @10. White eventually lost the game. Had White aimed the target right, he could have won. White should have played C2920 instead P1819? White would be in a winning situation with a major piece ahead in material.

1.7 EXECUTE EVERY MOVE WITH ACCURACY

Chess game is a mind game between two players. The one with a better plan, right target, correct strategy, and accurate execution should normally win the game. Accurate execution of moves is a very important key in winning a chess game. To execute every move without a mistake is not easy to accomplish in a chess game, particularly if your opponent is as good as you, or better.

1.8 DO NOT MAKE SERIOUS MISTAKES

It is impossible for any player not to make mistake in a chess game. We are human beings, not a computer. We can say this: a player who makes less fatal mistakes in a game, he will win the game.

2. SOME STRATEGIES USED WHEN YOU ARE DOWN

After evaluation of your situation, if you are down, you may have the following choices:

1. MAKE THE GAME AS COMPLICATED AS POSSIBLE

Don't make exchange of pieces, avoid the simplification strategy employed by your adversary. Intricate the situation and confuse your opponent to force him/her to make a mistake.

2. INITIATE COUNTER-ATTACK AND FIGHT TO THE END

You are down and a loss is inevitable, so with nothing to lose, why not take a chance with counter-attacks. The fierce fighting may bring you the chance to make a surprise checkmate one step faster than your adversary.

3. TRY TO SETTLE FOR A DRAW

Try to exchange the major pieces, wipe out the enemy Pawns and the defensive pieces, as many as possible. Arrange your defensive units correctly, and position your major pieces in strategic locations. Copy the standard draw positions you learn from Chapters 4 and 6: The Basic Endgame and the Special Rules.

4. FIND A WAY TO FORCE A DRAW

Take the advantage of the Legal Rules stated in Chapter 6 (The Special Rules). Force a drawn game by the Threefold Repetition draw rules. Games may be drawn if the readers are familiarized with the Endgames in Chapter 4 and the Special Rules in Chapter 6.

5. BE PATIENT AND WAIT FOR YOUR CHANCE

Keep cool and be patient. It is a very important skill and habit for player to have. Wait for your opponent to make mistake! Everyone makes mistakes. Any player makes mistakes.

6. ANNOYANCE OR DISTRCTION

Some players are very sensitive to annoyance caused by the opponent during the game, and mistake is made inevitably. This dirty tactics is not encouraged by the author. But, a chess player should learn how to cope with the situation if it happens. There are always some players try to win with all means.

7. HOPE THE GAME-TIME ON YOUR SIDE

When the time clock is used for the game, players should pay attention to the time during the game. Often, a player is ahead with pieces, but loses the game, due to the time pressure or exhaustion of his or her game time.

3. SOME STRATEGIES AND TACTICS OF THE MIDDLE GAME

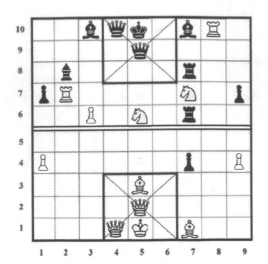

3.1. LOOKING AT THE BIG PICTURE

D 7.3.1

In this case, White is a major piece ahead and Black is desperately looking for a chance for a counterattack. The Black Cannon @28 wants to make a check, but the White Rook @27 stops it. White could have taken the Pawn @17 or the Bishop @30, he prefers to have the game in his control.

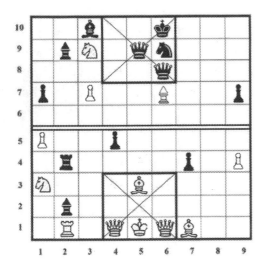

3.2. PINNING PIECES

D 7.3.2

In this case, White's Cannon @67 is pinning Black's King and Knight @69. Pinning down a Rook or King is one of the most beautiful ways in winning a chess game. The restrained Knight @69 is shielding the King from attack and its fate is doomed.

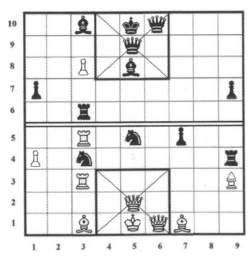

3.3. SIMPLIFY THE GAME WHEN AHEAD

D 7.3.3

Black, in this game, is a piece ahead and wants to simplify the game as much as possible to ensure an easy win. In this case, the Black Rook @36 from @26 is offering the exchange with the White Rook @35. Black figures out that he can win the game after the exchange. White would lose a valuable Pawn @38 if he declines it.

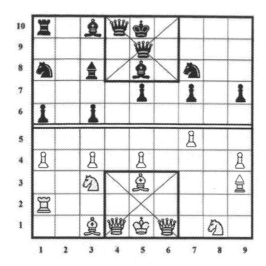

3.4. CONCENTRATION OF FORCES TO ATTACK

D 7.3.4

After the exchanges of the Rooks and Cannons in this case, Black's left flank is weak with one Knight @78 there. White mobilizes his Rook @12 and others to attack the weak flank. The game is always won by the side of greater forces in concentration (to attack an opponent's weak spot).

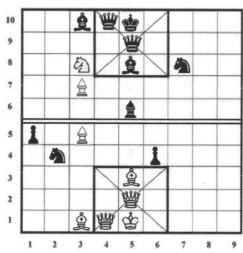

3.5. THE CHECKMATES

D 7.3.5

Whenever an opportunity is there for mate, don't let the winning chance go away! As we learn in Chapter 3 in this book, the "checkmates" can be very useful. In this case, White finds one. The Black Bishop @30 is the target for the two Cannons to attack (C3730+, C3530+) and mates.

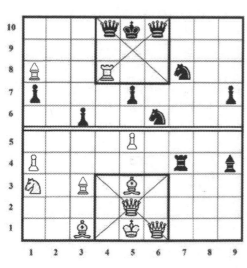

3.6. TAKE STRATEGIC SQUARES

D 7.3.6

The Black Rook, in this case, acts like a good midfielder in soccer game, takes the strategic square @74. There, he helps to protect the Knight @78, and provides the Cannon @94 an offense support.

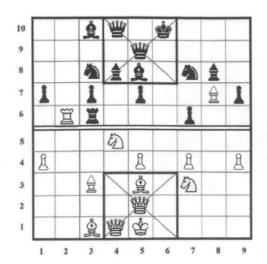

3.7. TEMPO GAINED FROM EXCHANGE OF PIECES

D 7.3.7

There are a few types of exchanges in a chess game. The most common one is "Exchange for a Gain". In this example, both sides are in equal pieces and values. But, White spots a Black's weakness in the unprotected Knight @38. He moves his Rook from @25 to @26 for an exchange of Rooks with the Black Rook @36. Whether the exchange is accepted or not, White would succeed his tactics.

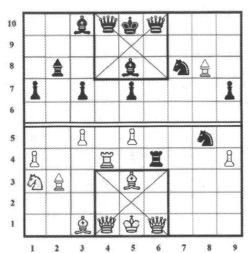

3.8. MOBILITY GAINED FROM EXCHANGE OF PIECES

D 7.3.8

In this case, both sides are equal in materials. The Black Rook @62 makes a move of R6264 to @64 and offers an exchange with White's Rook @44. The White Rook declines the offer, and Black succeeds his plan to take over the control of the vital 4th Rank with his Rook from @64, and White's right flank defense is completely exposed and subject to be attacked.

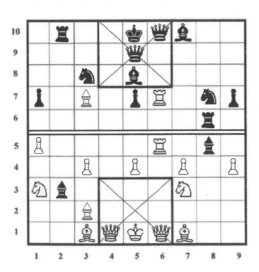

3.9. TARGET THE ROOKS

D 7.3.9

The Rooks, valued 5, is the most important piece in Chinese Chess. So the Rooks should be the top target, other than the King, of an attack. In this case, White carelessly puts both his two Rooks in dangerous positions shown in diagram. Black sees the opportunity and makes moves: 1----C2333, 2 C3733 N3846! Black gains a Rook.

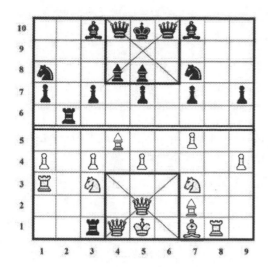

3.10. THE TRAPS

D 7.3.10

To have a piece ahead means a winning position most of the time in a chess game. To have a Rook ahead is almost a sure way to win the game in Chinese Chess. Here, in this case, the Black Rook @31 is trapped after taking the Bishop. It will be captured after B7153.

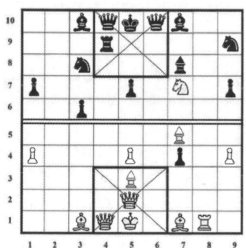

3.11. CAPTURE OF MAJOR PIECES

D 7.3.11

In this case, as shown in the diagram, White spots the falsely-protected Black Knight @99, a target for capture. White smartly succeeds his plan by: 1 C7555+ Q4059, 2 C5595 Q5940, 3 R8188 R4979, 4 C9599, and captures the Knight from the attack.

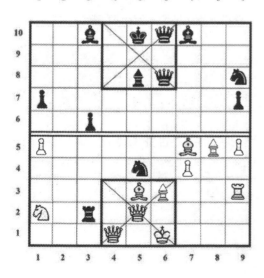

3.12. EXCHANGE OF A KNIGHT AND A CANNON FOR A ROOK

D 7.3.12

In Chinese Chess, it is advantageous in material most of the time with a Knight and a Cannon to exchange for a Rook. This is a case where White plays his Knight @12 to @33 and traps the Rook @32. The Black Rook would be caught by White's next move of C8582. Black is forced to make an exchange with his Rook for a Knight and a Cannon @63. White gains in the exchange.

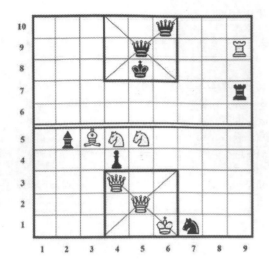

3.13. SACRIFICE OF PIECE(S) IN A MATE

D 7.3.13

Sacrifice of piece(s) to achieve a mate is always the most fascinating and enjoyable moves in a chess game. In this case, luckily it is White's turn to move and he makes R6999! The Rook @69 sacrifices itself to help the two Knights @55 and @45 to make a mate with N4537 and N5567.

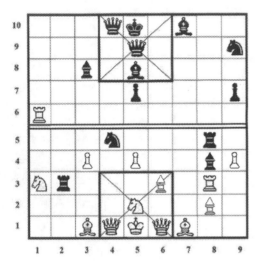

3.14. SACRIFICE A PIECE FIRST, GET EVEN LATER

D 7.3.14

When a piece of the same value can be gained back later, and then a piece can be sacrificed first. In this case, the Black's Rook @85 and Cannon @84 are pinned by the White Rook @83; and the White Rook @83 and Cannon @63 are pinned by the Black Rook @23 as well. When the entrapped Black Cannon is taken by the White Cannon, the White Rook @85 moves to @65 to gain back a piece of equal value.

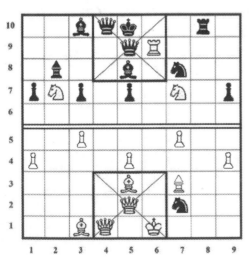

3.15. Advantage Gained from Sacrifice of Piece

D 7.3.15

In this case shown in D7.3.15, White sacrifices his Knight @77 first, taking the Black Bishop @58, threats to checkmate with N5839+. Black has to play B3058. White then plays C7378, gaining back a Black Knight @78, not afraid of Black's C2878 (White Knight @27 would checkmate with N2739+). Finally White's Cannon @78 forks Knight @72 and Cannon @28! and gains a huge advantage from the sacrifice.

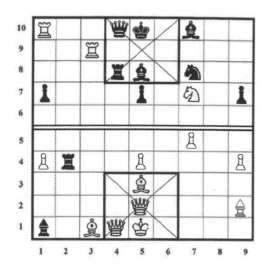

3.16. ALWAYS BE AGGRESSIVE

D 7.3.16

In this case, White does not take the advantage of "two Rooks against a single Queen" (an obvious weakness of defense structure in Chinese Chess). White should play an aggressive game by making the move of C9297, instead of the defensive play of R3933 he plays. White could have won the game if he plays more aggressively (R9297), rather a draw in actual play.

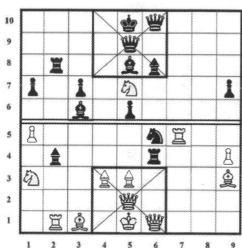

3.17. WATCH OUT ENEMY'S SURPRISE ATTACKS

D 7.3.17

In this case, after Black plays C6768 to secure the safety of Rook @28, White sees the Black's mating play C2454 and R6461#. The mating plan would have failed by White's move of R7565 if the Black Rook @28 is not protected first. White is a piece ahead and he understands to secure the defense before making an offense is the key. So White moves his Rook R7571 to prevent a mate.

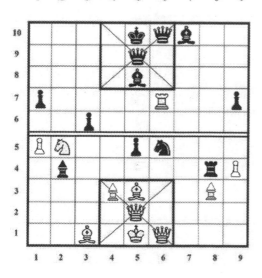

3.18. PREVENT ANY POTENTIAL COUNTER ATTACKS

D 7.3.18

In this case, Black is a major piece down and he tries to start the counter-attack moves. White of course will not let that happen and block the Black Cannon from making a check with moves: 1 C4323 C2494, 2 C8393, stopping Black any chance of counter attack.

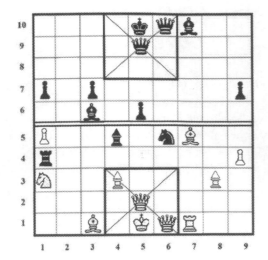

3.19. SOLIDIFY DEFENSE PRIOR TO ATTACK

7.3.19

A good defense is important to a sport team, as well as to a chess game. White is a major piece ahead in this case, he wants to solidify his defense before making an attack. So, he moves his Cannon out of the square @53 to give room for the connection of the Bishops, in solidification of the defense.

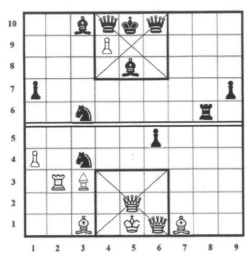

3.20. TAKE NO CHANCE WHEN YOU ARE IN SUPERIOR

D 7.3.20

Black is a piece ahead in this case. His Bishop @30 is unprotected since the White Pawn is at @49. Considering it is a weakness of the defense, Black moves the Bishop out to @18 from @30, to avoid the potential attack from the White Cannon @33. Also Black can free his two Knights @34 and @36 to launch an attack, without worry the defense.

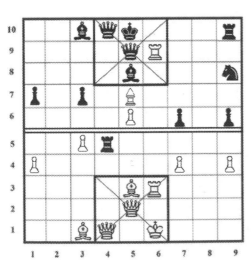

3.21. KING CAN HELP IN MATES

D 7.3.21

The diagram in this case indicates that Black is checkmated without any hope to save the fate, when White King moves out to @61 to help his two Rooks @63 and @69 to make the mate (1 R6960+ R9060, 2 R6360#). In many occasions, the King is used successfully to help in a mate.

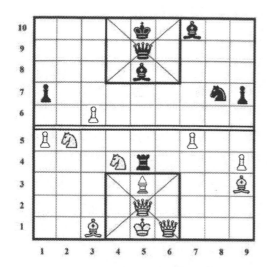

3.22. GET RID OF THE HOSTILE PAWNS WHENEVER POSSIBLE

D 7.3.22

A Pawn can be a game-changer, or it can decide a game's outcome. So in the mid-game phase, whenever possible, one should clear up the enemy's Pawn as many as possible. In this case, the Pawns are particular important to both sides. So each side takes one Pawn and the game ends up in a draw.

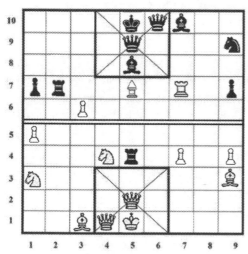

3.23. ONE QUEEN IS GAINED

D 7.3.23

A Queen is a part of the defense unit made up with two Queens and two Bishops. Missing a Queen or a Bishop is like missing a limb of a human body. When the defense unit is undermined, the defense is defective. In this case, a mistake by Black's move of R2027 costs him a Queen: 1 C5759! R2777, 2 C5954+ Q6059.

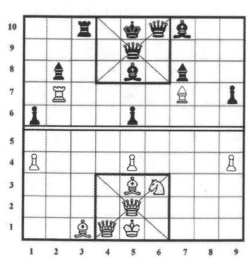

3.24. ONE BISHOP IS GAINED

D 7.3.24

This case shows a Black Bishop @70 will be lost with White's move of C7770+ B5870, R2728.

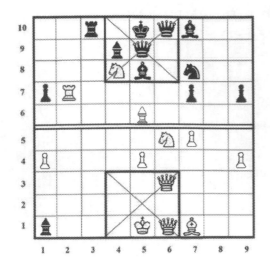

3.25. USE QUEENS WISELY

D 7.3.25

When under attack by a team of a Rook and a Cannon, a Queen should go up to the Palace corner-squares to side-step the dangerous attack, a very effective defense tactics, as shown in the diagram (White Queen @63). One condition to use this defensive tactics is to make sure there is no 3rd major hostile piece around to involve in this attack.

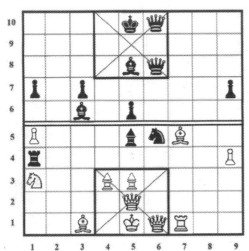

3.26 THE BISHOPS CAN BE HELPFUL

D 7.3.26

One very useful defensive tactics for the Bishops is to block the invading Knight at the border line, as shown in the diagram. White Bishop @75 blocks the Black Knight to @84.

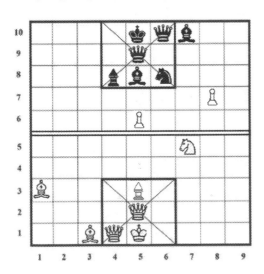

3.27. A PAWN CAN MAKE THE DIFFERENCE

D 7.3.27

The Pawns are not powerful while they are still in their own territory. They become more powerful after crossing the border line into the enemy territory. A Pawn or two ahead in the mid-games can decide the winner of a game. When one has two Pawns ahead in the mid-game phase, the tactic "Win with Pawns ahead" can be applied. In this case, as shown in D7.3.27, White has two Pawns ahead and should win with a careful approach.

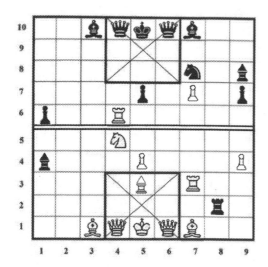

3.28. INITIATE COUNTER ATTACKS AND FIGHT TO THE END

D 7.3.28

The diagram shows a loss for White is inevitable, since he is a major piece down. Backing against the wall, he determines to fight it back hard. And he succeeds in this case with moves as follows:

1 ---R8782, 2 N4566 R3031, 3 N6678 C1411, 4 R7363 Q6059, 5 C5357+ Q5968, 6 R6343 R3130, 7 Q4052 and White wins after 8 K5141.

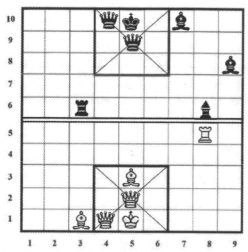

3.29. SETTLE FOR A DRAW

D 7.3.29

This diagram shows White is a major piece down. He has no chance to win and attempts to settle with a draw. There are many draw situations illustrated in Chapters 4 and 6. In this case, the Black Cannon @86 is a protected piece, the white Rook @85 can perpetual attack the Cannon @86 without violation of the rules. It would be a draw still if the Rook first captured the Cannon and then allowed to be captured himself (Because a Rook alone cannot defeat an experienced player with a full defense unit of two Queens and two Bishops). See Page 97, D4.12.1.

3.30. FORCE A DRAW

D 7.3.30

This diagram indicates Black has chances to win and White has no chance at all. Fortunately for White, he can force a draw by one of the rules stated in Chapter 6. The Rule states that: Perpetual Blocking is legal and a permissible move. The two Cannons @23 and @83 are protecting each other, and move along the 3rd rank to block the Black Rook @84 to escape a mate.

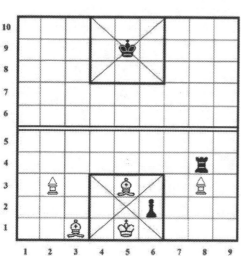

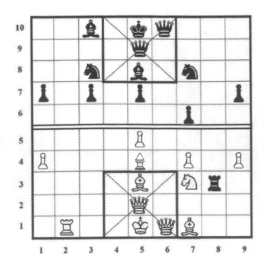

3.31. PIECE SAVING

D 7.3.31

The diagram D7.3.31 shows that the Black Rook @83 is attacking the unprotected Knight @73, and the Knight has no place to escape. White's Cannon @54 skillfully makes an attack on the unprotected Black Knight @38, and let the endangered Knight @73 escape to the safe and empty square @54. By doing that, the Knight is saved.

3.32. PLAN AHEAD A DRAW

When a player faces an opponent of much higher ranking in a tournament game, or a draw from the specific game will make you or your team a championship, he/she may use this tactic to get a draw and split the point out of the game. The strategies and tactics you should play for a draw are: 1) Play aggressively. 2) Have a draw in mind. 3) Make exchanges of pieces as early and as much as possible, particular the powerful Rooks. 4) Wipe out the hostile Pawns and save your own as many as possible. 5) Undermine the opponent defense (the Queens and Bishops) and keep yours intact as much as possible 6) Take advantage of the rules and the Threefold Repetition to obtain a draw. 7) To simplify the game so that your adversary is unable to mate you.

3.33. MAKE THE GAME AS COMPLICATED AS POSSIBLE

When you are down, you don't want to take a quick withdrawal. Most accomplished chess players are determined and proud fighters. You have to believe in yourself and don't give up until the last move of the game. So, why not make the game as complicated and confused as much as possible, so that your enemy gets confused and may make a stupid mistake. Then, you can regain the momentum and may turn the table around and win the game.

3.34. WAIT FOR YOUR CHANCE TO COME

We are human. Human makes mistakes. And your adversary is a human and he or she will make mistakes. There are mistakes and opportunities in every game, a beginner's or professional's.

3.35. ANNOYANCE OR DISTRACTION

This tactics is not recommended but our readers and players should be aware of this dirty tactic. There are always some players who try to win a game and points with every means and at any cost.

3.36. HOPE THE TIME IS ON YOUR SIDE

The game time can be a player's night-mare. On the other hands, when you are not doing well in a game, the "Time" might be your best and lovely friends. Time pressure can also cause one to make mistakes.

CHAPTER 8   SOME GRAND MASTER GAMES

GAME NO. 1   YANG GUAN-LIN VS. LI YI-TING (2003)

59 Cannons vs. Rook Exchange Declined

1.	C8353	N8078
2.	N8173	R9080
3.	R9181	P7776
4.	R8187	N2038
5.	P3435	C8898
6.	R8777	C9899
7.	N2133	Q4059
8.	C2313	C9979
9.	R7767 (1)	N7886
10.	R1121	R1020
11.	N3345	P7675
12.	R6769	C7974
13.	B7193	C7484
14.	N4557	N3857
15.	C5357+	B3058
16.	R2126	P7574
17.	C1323 (2)	P7473
18.	R2666	N8678
19.	C2320	N7866
20.	R6966	C8481+
21.	B9371	R8084
22.	R6656	P1716
23.	Q4152	C2848
24.	P3536	P7372
25.	P3637	P7262
26.	P3738	R8482
27.	R5646 (3)	R8272
28.	R4648	
	Black resigned	

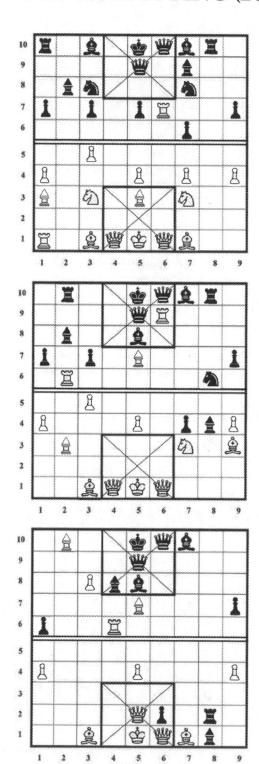

197

GAME NO. 2   LI YI-TING VS. YANG GUAN-LIN (1963)

57 Cannons vs. Rook Exchange Declined

56.	R2050	K6968
57.	R5059	
	Black resigned	

1.	C8353	N8078
2.	N8173	R9080
3.	R9181	N2038
4.	P3435	P7776
5.	R8187	C8898
6.	R8777	C9899
7.	C2333 (1)	C9979
8.	R7767	Q4059
9.	P5455	N7886
10.	R6764	R8088
11.	N2113	R1020
12.	R1121	C2825
13.	P5556	P5756
14.	P1415	C2522
15.	Q4152	N8674
16.	K5141	B3058
17.	P3536	R8868
18.	R6468	Q5968
19.	P3637	N3840
20.	N7354	P5655
21.	N5435	R2024
22.	C3332	N7453
23.	B3153	C7929
24.	K4151	P5545
25.	N3547	Q6059
26.	Q5241	P7675
27.	C3282	P7574
28.	N4739+	K5060
29.	C8287 (2)	B5830
30.	C8767+	N4069
31.	N3947	P7473
32.	Q4152	B3058
33.	P3738	C2927
34.	C6766	C2726
35.	P3839	C2646
36.	C6667	R2423
37.	N4759	C4656
38.	N5938	R2313
39.	P3949	R1333
40.	N3846	K6050
41.	K5141	C2223
42.	C6769	C5654
43.	N4665	C5444
44.	N6544	P4544
45.	C6989	P4434
46.	K4151	P3424
47.	C8980+	B7098
48.	R2141	C2313
49.	R4148	B9876
50.	R4828	K5060
51.	R2820+	K6069
52.	C8030 (3)	C1311
53.	C3039+	Q6859
54.	K5141	R3331+
55.	K4142	R3134

198

GAME NO. 3   WANG JIA-LIANG
VS. YANG GUAN-LIN (1999)

Filed Rook vs. Knight Counter Attack

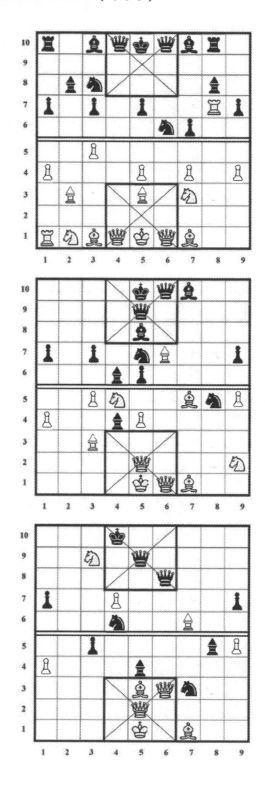

1.	C8353	N8078
2.	N8173	R9080
3.	R9181	N2038
4.	P3435	P7776
5.	R8187	N7866 (1)
6.	N2133	B3058
7.	C5363	Q4059
8.	R8785	P7675
9.	R8575	C8878
10.	B3153	R1040
11.	Q4152	C2824
12.	R1141	R4041+
13.	K5141	R8085
14.	N7392	C7874
15.	R7585	N6685
16.	N3345	C2434
17.	C2333	C7476
18.	P9495	C7646+
19.	K4151	P5756
20.	B5375	N3857
21.	C6367	C3444 (2)
22.	C6764	C4442
23.	C3353	C4292
24.	C5356	N8573
25.	P5455	C9282
26.	C5658+	B7058
27.	P5556	C8285
28.	N4533	C8535
29.	C6474	C4636
30.	N3345	N5738
31.	B7153	C3525
32.	Q5263	Q5968
33.	P5646	C3634
34.	P4647	P3736
35.	N4566	C2555+
36.	Q6152	C3464
37.	N6658	Q6059
38.	B7593	C6454
39.	N5839+	K5040
40.	B9371	P3635
41.	C7478	N3846
42.	C7876	C5585 (3)
43.	B7193	C8581
44.	C7686	N7392
45.	C8682	N4665
46.	N3958	N6584
47.	K5141	P3534
48.	N5846	P3444
49.	N4625	P4434
50.	N2546	P3444
51.	N4625	N8465
52.	B9375	N9284
53.	C8283	C5474
54.	P4737	C7471+
55.	K4142	C7172+
56.	K4241	C7262
57.	K4151	P4454
58.	N2533	C6292
59.	Q5241	N8463+
	White resigned	

GAME NO. 4   LIU DIAN-ZHONG
VS. WANG JIA-LING (1988)

57 Cannons vs. Cannon Blocking

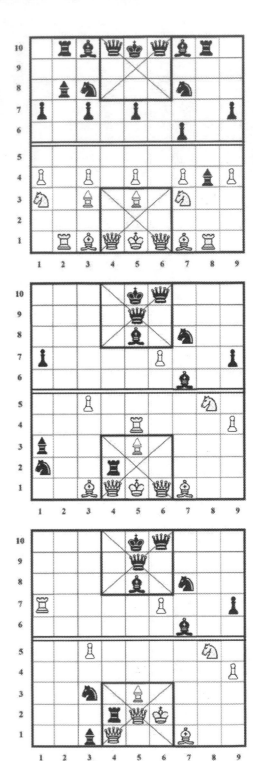

1.	C8353	N8078
2.	N8173	R9080
3.	R9181	N2038
4.	N2113	P7776
5.	C2333	R1020
6.	R1121	C8884 (1)
7.	R2127	C2818
8.	R2737	R2028
9.	R3735	B3058
10.	P7475	N3826
11.	P7576	N2614
12.	R3585	R8085
13.	N7385	N1433
14.	R8184	B5876
15.	P5455	R2822
16.	P3435	N3312
17.	P5556	C1813
18.	P5657+	Q4059
19.	P5767	B7058
20.	R8454	R2242 (2)
21.	Q6152	N1231
22.	R5414	C1333
23.	R1417	N3112
24.	K5161	C3331+
25.	K6162	N1233 (3)
26.	K6263	C3135
27.	N8564	N3354
28.	C5358+	K5040
29.	R1714	N7866
30.	N6456	N5475+
31.	K6353	N7556
32.	C5888	Q5968
33.	C8880+	Q6059
34.	C8089	C3530
35.	C8986	R4212
36	R1434	R1232
37	R3432	N6573+
38	K5363	N5544+
	White resigned	

200

GAME NO. 5   HU RONG-HUA VS. YANG KUAN -LIN (1964)

58 Cannons vs. Rook Counter Attack

1.	C8353	N8078
2.	P7475	P3736
3.	C2327	R9080
4.	N8173	C8898 (1)
5.	N2133	B3058
6.	C2777	N2038
7.	R1121	C2826
8.	R2125	P1716
9.	P3435	P3635
10.	R2535	N3846
11.	N3345	R8087
12.	C7770+	B5870
13.	R3536	C2623
14.	R3646	C2373
15.	R9193	C7374
16.	R9373	C7414
17.	P7576 (2)	R1030
18.	P7677	R8782
19.	N4566	R3031
20.	N6678	C1411
21.	R7363	Q6059
22.	C5357+	Q5968
23.	R6343	R3130+
24.	Q4152	R8288
25.	K5141	C9878
26.	R4640+	R3040
27.	R4340+	K5059
28.	R4049+	K5950
29.	B7153(3)	C1121
30.	R4940+	K5059
31.	R4070	C2128
32.	R7079+	K5950
33.	P7767	C2826
34.	P5455	C2676
35.	R7969	C7666
36.	C5756	C7876
37.	C5676	R8887
38.	P5556	R8767
39.	P5666	R6766
40.	C7673	R6664
41.	R6949	R6494
42.	R4940+	K5059
43.	R4047	K5950
44.	B5371	P1615
45.	R4757+	Q6859
46.	C7353	R9444+
47.	K4151	K5040
48.	R5759	R4442
49.	R5955	
	Black resigned	

GAME NO. 6   CAI FU-RU VS. HU RONG HUA (1960)

Filed Rook vs. Knight Counter Attack

1.	C8353	N8078
2.	N8173	P7776
3.	R9181	R9080
4.	R8187	N2038
5.	P3435	N7866
6.	N2133	B7058
7.	P5455 (1)	P7675
8.	R8767	N6674
9.	P5556	Q4059
10.	N7354	C8883
11.	P5657	C2827
12.	P3536	C8333
13.	P3637	R8084
14.	N5433	C2757+
15.	Q4152	N7455
16.	R6766	C5777
17.	C5373	C7773
18.	C2373	N3857
19.	N3325	R1020
20.	N2546	N5745
21.	R6662	R2022
22.	R1113	R8434
23.	B3153	R3444
24.	R1333	R2221+
25.	B5331	R4442
26.	R3335	N4553 (2)
27.	N4654	R4244
28.	R6263	N5334
29.	R6333	R4454
30.	C7383	R5484
31.	C8393	R8494
32.	P3738	R2126
33.	P3839	R2636
34.	R3545	R9496
35.	C9383	R9686
36.	P3949	P7565
37.	R4544	N3426
38.	R3336	N5536
39.	R4443	N2634
40.	R4323	Q5940
41.	C8333	B3018
42.	R2325	N3655
43.	R2528	B1836
44.	C3323	R8646
45.	R2829	B3618
46.	R2939	R4626
47.	C2383	R2621
48.	B7153	N3453
49.	R3933	N5372+
50.	K5141	Q6059
51.	K4142	R2124
52.	R3373	R2422+
53.	K4241	R2221
54.	R7333	R2126
55.	R3373	R2636 (3)
	White resigned	

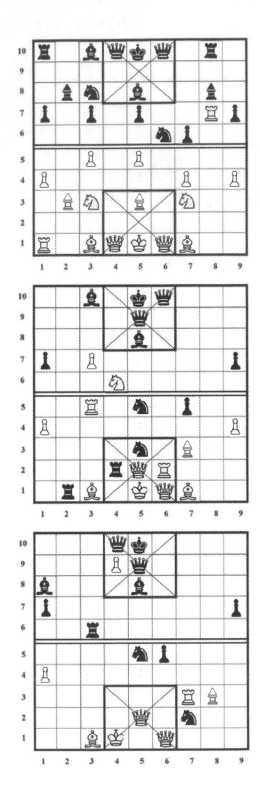

GAME NO. 7   CAI FU-RU VS. HU RONG-HUA (1964)

57 Cannons vs. Knight's Gambit Declined

1.	C8353	N8078
2.	N8173	R9080
3.	R9181	P7776
4.	R8187	N2038
5.	P3435	Q4059
6.	C2333	B3058
7.	P3536 (1)	B5836
8.	R8777	C8889
9.	N2113	C8979
10.	R7767	N7886
11.	R1121	R1020
12.	R6765	C2824
13.	P5455	B7058
14.	P1415	C7974
15.	B7093	P7675
16.	R6575	R8070
17.	R7585	R7076
18.	Q4152	R7666
19.	P5556	P5756
20.	N7354	R6664
21.	N5446	N8665
22.	N4638	R2028
23.	N3857	C7477
24.	R8575	C7767 (2)
25.	C3343	C6768
26.	R7571	C2454
27.	N5776	R2821
28.	N7668+	Q5968
29.	N1321	C5455
30.	N2113	R6414
31.	B9375	Q6859
32.	K5141	C5545+
33.	K4151	B5870
34.	C5383	R1484
35.	B7553	B3658
36.	R7179	C4544
37.	R7969	P5655
38.	R6967	P3736
39.	N1325	C4424
40.	C4323	C2494
41.	C8393 (3)	P3635
42.	N2537	R8424
43.	N3756	P3545
44.	R6717	R2420
45.	P1516	C9454
46.	N5675	B5876
47.	R1797	C5414
48.	C2326	C1411+
49.	Q5241	R2028
50.	R9737	P5554
51.	C2656+	Q5948
52.	C9395	N6553
53.	R7757+	Q6059
54.	R5727+	
	Black resigned	

GAME NO. 8   HU RONG- HUA VS. LV QIN (2001)

Bishop Opening vs. Pawn Defense

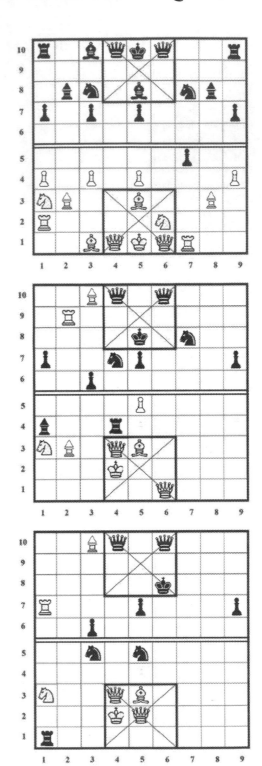

1.	B7153	P7776
2.	N2113	N8078
3.	R1112	B7058
4.	N8162	N2038
5.	P7475	P7675
6.	R9171 (1)	N7866
7.	R7175	R9070
8.	R7570	B5870
9.	P3435	N3859
10.	R1242	N5978
11.	C8373	B7058
12.	R4244	R1019
13.	P5455	N6685
14.	C7383	R1969
15.	C8388	R6962
16.	Q4152	R6264
17.	R4449	N8566
18.	P3536	P3736
19.	C2333	B3013
20.	C8858	C2824
21.	R4948	C2494
22.	C5818	R6474
23.	K5141	C9491+
24.	K4142	Q4059
25.	R4838	R7444+
26.	Q5243	C9131
27.	R3830+	Q5940
28.	R3020	C3111
29.	C1310	K5059
30.	R2029+	K5958
31.	C3323	C1114
32.	C1030	N6647 (2)
33.	C2324	N7866
34.	R2927	N4755
35.	Q6152	K5868
36.	N1332	R4484
37.	C2421	N6647
38.	R2717	C1434
39.	C3034	R8434
40.	N3213	R3431
41.	C2120	R3111
42.	C2030	N4735 (3)
43.	Q5263	N3523+
44.	K4252	R1112+
45.	K5251	N5543+
46.	K5161	N2342+
47.	K6151	N4221+
48.	K5161	R1213
	White resigned	

GAME NO. 9   LV QIN VS. LI LAI-QUN (1994)

58 Cannons vs. Bishop Defense

1.	C8353	N8078
2.	N8173	R9080
3.	R9181	N2038
4.	P7475	P3736
5.	N2113	B3058
6.	C2327 (1)	P7776
7.	P7576	B5876
8.	C2797	C2823
9.	N7365	C8883
10.	C9777	B7658
11.	R1112	R1019
12.	R1222	R1969
13.	N6557	N3857
14.	C5357+	N7857
15.	R2223	C8382
16.	C7717	R6964 (2)
17.	C1710+	B5830
18.	R2353	N5765
19.	Q4152	R6474
20.	R5363	N6573
21.	R8191	C8283
22.	R6362	N7354
23.	B3153	C8381
24.	R6268	R8082
25.	R6848	Q6059
26.	R4838	R8252+(3)
27.	K5152	N5473+
28.	K5251	R7464
	White resigned	

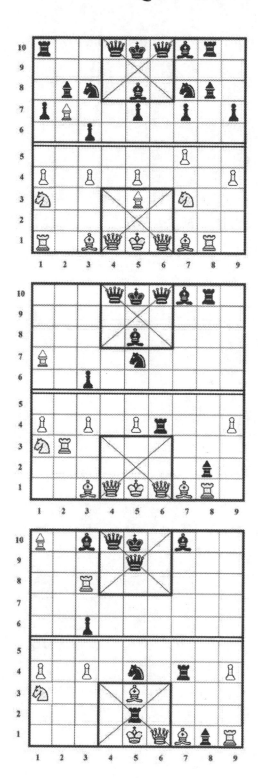

GAME NO. 10   LI LAI-QUN VS. LIU DA-HUA (1984)

Bishop Opening vs. Cannon Center Defense

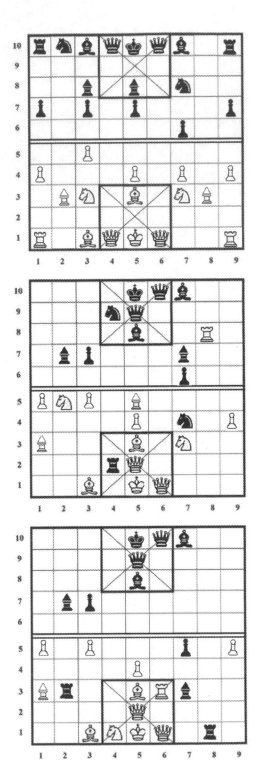

1.	B7153	C8858
2.	N2133	N8078
3.	N8173	P7776
4.	P3435	C2838 (1)
5.	N3325	R9080
6.	R9181	N7866
7.	Q4152	N6674
8.	P1415	C5878
9.	R1114	B3058
10.	R1444	R8085
11.	C2313	N2018
12.	N2517	C3848
13.	R4424	R1020
14.	R2420	N1820
15.	C8393	R8545
16.	C9397	R4542
17.	R8187	Q4059
18.	C9757	C4828
19.	N1725	N2049
20.	C5755	C2827
21.	R8788	C7877 (2)
22.	R8885	R4222
23.	C5545	N4957
24.	N2533	R2223
25.	N3341	N5745
26.	R8545	N7493
27.	R4565	C7773
28.	R6563	N9381
29.	P9495	P7675 (3)
	White resigned	

GAME NO. 11   XU YIN-CHUAN
VS. LIU DA-HUA (1998)

57 Cannons vs. Cannon Blocking

1.	C8353	N8078
2.	N8173	R9080
3.	R9181	N2038
4.	P7475	P3736
5.	C2333	Q4059
6.	N2113	N3826
7.	R1112	B3058
8.	R1242	C8884
9.	N7365	C8434
10.	R8180	C3431+
11.	Q4152	N7880
12.	R4247	C2838
13.	R4727 (1)	C3833
14.	R2726	C3111
15.	N1332	C1112
16.	R2623	C3335
17.	C5357	N8078
18.	C5756	C3545
19.	R2327	C4540
20.	N3224	C1211
21.	N2436	R1030
22.	N3648+	C4049
23.	Q5263	C1112
24.	B7153	C1282
25.	Q6152	C8288
26.	N6577	N7857 (2)
27.	R2757	C8848
28.	R5717	R3034
29.	R1718	C4838
30.	P5455	C4942
31.	R1310+	C3830
32.	R1017	C4244
33.	N7789	C3038
34.	R1767	K5040
35.	R6747+(3)	C3848
36.	N8960	C4474
37.	C5659	K4050
38.	R4748	K5059
39.	N6049	R3439
40.	R4844	C7473
41.	K5141	C7353
42.	P5556	
	Black resigned	

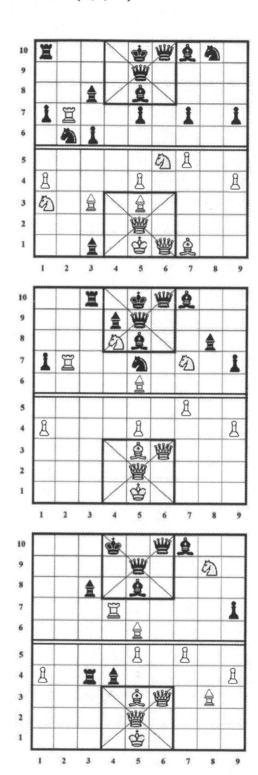

GAME NO. 12   YU YOU HUA VS.
XU YIN CHUAN (2001)

57 Cannons vs. Cannon Border Defense

1.	C8353	N8078
2.	N8173	R9080
3.	R9181	N2038
4.	N2113	P7776
5.	C2333	R1020
6.	R1121	C2826 (1)
7.	R8187	N7766
8.	R2125	B3058
9.	P1415	Q4059
10.	C3337	P7675
11.	R8767	C8885
12.	R2575	R8086
13.	R7565	N6687
14.	C5333	C2623
15.	C3332	C2333
16.	C3733	N3846
17.	C3282	C8575
18.	P7475	N4665
19.	N7365	R8682
20.	R6777	R2026
21.	C3353	R8285
22.	B7193	R2666
23.	N6573	R8584
24.	Q4152	N8799
25.	C5357	R6656
26.	N7365	R8464
27.	N6544	R5626
28.	P3435	R6454
29.	P3536	R2627
30.	C5759 (2)	R2777
31.	C5954+	R7757
32.	C5453	Q6059
33.	N1325	R5754
34.	P3646	N9987
35.	C5313	R5494
36.	B3153	P9796
37.	B9371	R9454
38.	C1317	P9695
39.	P4656	R5464
40.	C1737	P9585
41.	C3734	R6468
42.	B7193	R6898
43.	C3433	R9894
44.	P1516	N8768
45.	P5646	N6887
46.	P1617	R9454
47.	B9371	P8575
48.	P1727	P7574
49.	C3334	R5457
50.	P2737	N8795
51.	P4647	R5767
52.	N2546	R6766
53.	N4465	R6656
54.	C3436	R5655
55.	N6577	N9576

56.	N4667	R5565
57.	N6779+	K5060
58.	N7987	R6567
59.	N7789+	K6050
60.	N8968+ (3)	K5060
61.	C3666	Q5968
62.	P4757	R6766
63.	N8766	P7464
64.	P5767	Q6859
65.	K5141	N7688
66.	P6777	N8896
67.	P7778	N9675
68.	P3738	N7556
69.	P3839	B5876
70.	P7879	Q5948
71.	N6678	N5668
72.	N7897	N6887
73.	P7989	N8768
	A Draw	

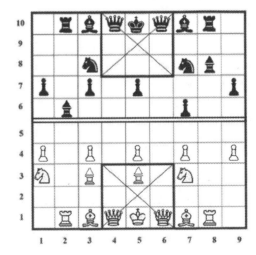

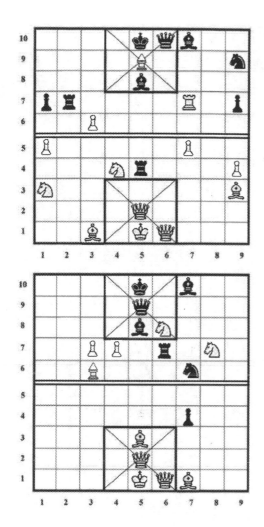

GAME NO. 13   XU YIN-CHUAN
VS. YU YOU-HUA (2001)

57 Cannons vs. Cannon Blocking

1.	C8353	N8078
2.	N8173	R9080
3.	R9181	N2038
4.	N2113	P7776
5.	C2333	R1020
6.	R1121	C8884
7.	R2127	C2818
8.	R2737	R2028 (1)
9.	R3735	B3058
10.	P7475	N3826
11.	R3525	P7675
12.	R2575	N2514
13.	C3332	R2823
14.	C3272	C1838
15.	N7352	N7899
16.	R7515	P1716 (2)
17.	R1516	N1426
18.	R8183	Q6059
19.	C7282	N2645
20.	C5363	R8085
21.	C8284	N9987
22.	R1615	N8775 (3)
23.	R1545	R8584
24.	B3153	N7563+
25.	R8363	R2313
	A Draw	

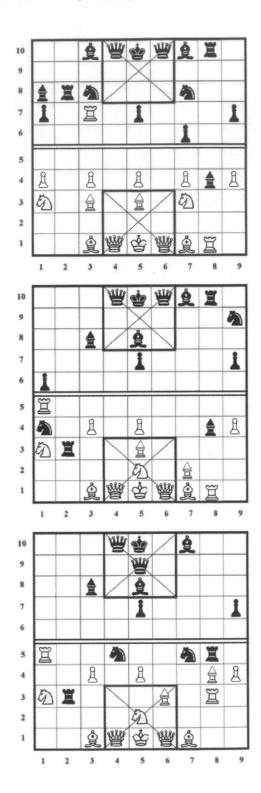

GAME NO. 14   ZHAO GUA-RONG
VS. XU YIN-CHUAN (1998)

Pawn Opening vs. Cannon Defense

1.	P3435	C2838
2.	C8353	B3058
3.	N8173	R9099
4.	C5357+ (1)	Q4059
5.	B3153	N2049
6.	C5756	R9969
7.	P7475	N8078
8.	N2142	N4957
9.	R9181	C8898
10.	P5455	R6964
11.	N4254	R1020
12.	C2333	R2024
13.	R1131	P7776
14.	C3334	R6462
15.	Q4152	P7675
16.	N5475	N5776
17.	R8187	N7857
18.	C3454	C9878
19.	R8777	C3828
20.	C5658+	B7058
21.	P5556	C2827
22.	P5657	N7657
23.	N7556	C7873
24.	C5457	C2757
25.	R7757	R2428
26.	N5637 (2)	R6268
27.	R3141	P9796
28.	N3749	R2838
29.	R5717	R3830
30.	N4928	R3038
31.	R1710+	B5830
32.	N2830	Q5940
33.	N3019	R3848
34.	R4148	R6848
35.	N1927	R4847
36.	N2739+	R4749
37.	N3927	Q6059
38.	R1016	R4929
39.	N2746	R2921+
40.	Q5241	R2124
41.	N4658 (3)	
	Black resigned	

GAME NO. 15   XU TIAN-HONG
VS. ZHAO GUA-RONG (1995)

Cannons Game

1.	C8353	C8858
2.	N8173	N8078
3.	R9181	P7776
4.	N2133	N2038
5.	P3435	R1019
6.	C2325	R1949
7.	P7475	R4946
8.	N7365	R4643
9.	R1113	P7675
10.	Q6152	R4342
11.	N6577	P7574
12.	N3345	R9099
13.	N4566	R9949
14.	P3536 (1)	P3736
15.	C2575	R4246
16.	R1343	R4643
17.	Q5243	N7899
18.	Q4352	C5878
19.	N6678	C2878
20.	C7555+	Q4059
21.	C5595	Q5940
22.	R8188	R4979
23.	C9599	P7464
24.	B7193	P6454
25.	C5333	B3058
26.	C9990	N3846
27.	N7785	C7874
28.	N8566	P5444
29.	C3353	C7454
30.	N6654	P4454
31.	C5357+	Q4059
32.	R8868	K5040
33.	C5759 (2)	K4049
34.	C5950	R7999
35.	R6860	K4959
36.	R6066	N4638
37.	R6667	B7098
38.	R6737	R9990
39.	R3738	K5950
40.	R3858+	K5060
41.	R5854	R9099
42.	R5457 (3)	P1716
43.	R5797	R9989
44.	B9371	R8984
45.	R9798	R8414
46.	P9495	R1474
47.	R9868+	K6050
48.	R6858+	K5040
49.	R5856	P3635
50.	R5616	
	Black resigned	

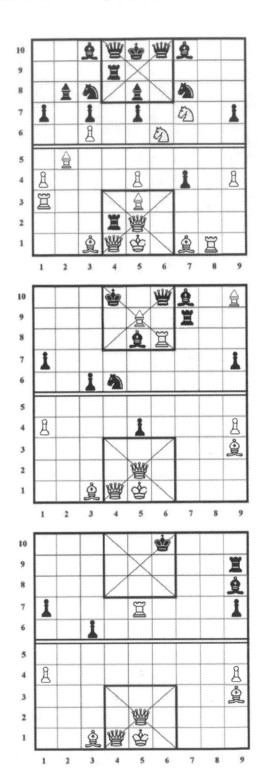

GAME NO. 16   TAO HAN-MING
VS. XU TIAN-HONG (1997)

Cannons Game

1.	C8353	C8858
2.	N8173	N8078
3.	R9181	P7776
4.	N2133	N2038
5.	P3435	C2824
6.	N3345	C2474
7.	C2333	R1020
8.	N4537 (1)	C5848
9.	Q6152	R2024
10.	N3745	R2434
11.	P3536	N3846
12.	P3646	C4845
13.	R1113	Q6059
14.	P4647	C4575
15.	P5455	P9796
16.	R8184	R3464
17.	C3337 (2)	B7058
18.	C5357	R9060
19.	C5767	R6080
20.	R8480+	N7880
21.	P5556	N8069
22.	P5657	N6988
23.	P1415	C7471
24.	R1363	C7555+
25.	R4353	N8867
26.	P5767	C5525
27.	R5354	R6462
28.	R5455	C2527
29.	P4757	C7191
30.	C3732	R6264
31.	R5554	R6466
32.	P5758	K5060
33.	Q5243	R6663
34.	R5484 (3)	B3058
35.	R8480+	K6069
36.	C3239+	
	Black resigned	

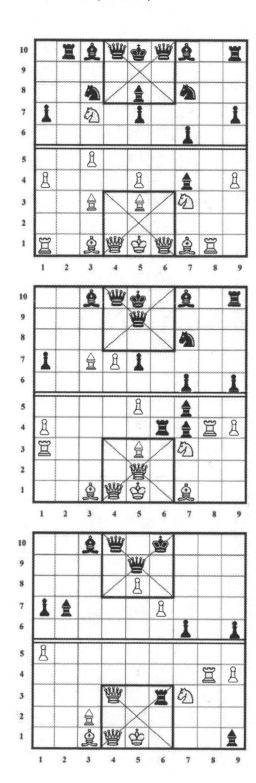

GAME NO. 17   LIU DIAN-ZHONG
VS. TAO HAN-MING (2001)

57 Cannons vs. Cannon Blocking

1.	C8353	N2038
2.	N8173	N8078
3.	R9181	R9080
4.	N2113	P7776
5.	C2333	R1020
6.	R1121	C8884
7.	R2127	C2818
8.	R2737	R2028 (1)
9.	R3735	N3826
10.	R3525	N2647
11.	R2545	N4726
12.	C3330+	Q4059
13.	R4535	C1814
14.	R8182	R2848
15.	P7475	P7675
16.	R3575	C8474
17.	R8280	C7471+
18.	Q6152	C7175
19.	R8085	C7574
20.	R8535	B7058
21.	C3020	P1716
22.	P5455	N2638
23.	C2023	N3846
24.	P5556	P5756
25.	C2343	N4638
26.	R3537	C7454
27.	K5161	N7886
28.	P3435	C1415
29.	R3777	N8665
30.	N7365	C1565
31.	C4347 (2)	C5464+
32.	K6151	B5870
33.	C4757+	K5040
34.	R774	R4844
35.	C5343+	R4414
36.	C5747+	K4050
37.	C4373	B7058
38.	C4787 (3)	C6454+
39.	B3153	K5040
40.	C8784	N3746
41.	P3536	P1615
42.	C8480+	K4049
43.	P3646	P5655
44.	R7477	
	Black resigned	

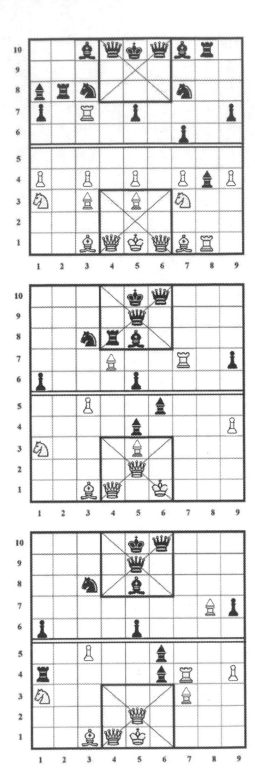

GAME NO. 18 ZHAO GUA-RONG VS. LV QIN (1991)

59 Cannons vs. Rook Exchange Declined

1.	C8353	N8078
2.	N8173	R9080
3.	R9181	N2038
4.	P3435	P7775
5.	R8187	C8898
6.	R8777	C9899
7.	N2133	Q4059
8.	C2313	R1020
9.	R1121	C9979
10.	R7767	N7886
11.	R6769	C7974
12.	B7193	C2824
13.	P5455	P7675
14.	B9375	C7434
15.	P5556	P5756
16.	N3354 (1)	R8088
17.	N5446	C3414
18.	Q6152	N8674
19.	R2123	N3840
20.	P3536	N4058
21.	N4638	R2028
22.	C1317	N7453
23.	B7553	P3736
24.	C1710+	Q5940
25.	N3857	N5877
26.	R6979	N7765 (2)
27.	R2343	R2820
28.	N5776	R8818
29.	C1030+	R2030
30.	N7365	B7098
31.	R7929	B9876
32.	R2924	R3037
33.	R4346	P5655
34.	R4656+	R1858 (3)
35.	R5658+	B7658
36.	R2414	P5565
37.	R1415	
	A Draw	

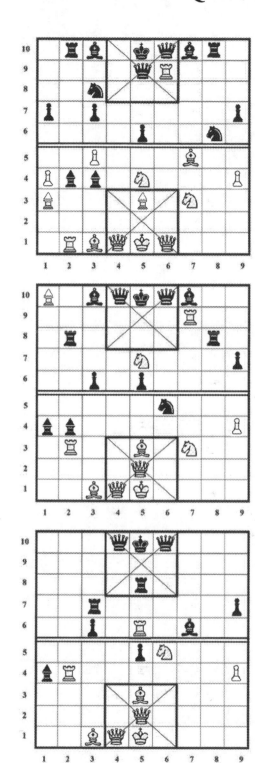

215

Printed in the United States
By Bookmasters